Popper

The Champion Guides

Rafe Champion

CONTENTS

PREFACE

Karl Popper lived a long and productive life, leaving a score of books including at least two of which are classics, namely *The Logic of Scientific Discovery* and *The Open Society and Its Enemies*. He made contributions to many areas of thought and he deserves to be a household name among educated people. This is not the case, although a lay readership is keeping *The Open Society and Its Enemies* in print.

These guides are written for busy people who are daunted by the prospect of reading a shelf of books, with the risk that they will start with *The Logic of Scientific Discovery* which is not a book for beginners. They are designed to provide an access to the key ideas and themes in five particularly important books.

The Logic of Scientific Discovery first appeared in German as *Logik Der Forschung* (1935). It was a game-changing book in the philosophy of science, introducing a cluster of significant ideas including conjectural knowledge, working without foundations and the role of social conventions or rules of the game of science. It stands as a critique of the central ideas of logical positivism and logical empiricism which dominated the philosophy of science through most of the 20th century.

The Open Society and Its Enemies, first published in 1945, challenged several schools of thought; on the conservative side the admirers of Plato and Aristotle; on the other side the adherents of Hegel and Marx. Popper did not belittle the achievements of Plato, and Marx, indeed he paid them generous compliments while he directed his critical attention on ideas which confuse and divide the friends of freedom, making way for totalitarian regimes in the 20th century and beyond.

Arthur Koestler described *The Poverty of Historicism* (1957) as the one book published that year that would outlast the century. It demolished the deterministic or "locomotive" theory of history that everything happens according to some pre-determined plan regardless of our efforts to obtain different outcomes. It contains the first version of Popper's ideas about situational analysis and the rationality principle which he located at the core of social and historical analysis. He drew attention to the importance of the social and institutional context for economic and scientific progress.

Conjectures and Refutations (1963) is a showcase of Popper's wide-ranging contributions through the 1950s. Some of these papers are classics, especially "On the Sources of Knowledge and of Ignorance" where he demonstrated the political significance of ideas about the foundations of knowledge.

Objective Knowledge (1972) contains an exciting series of papers which demonstrate the evolutionary and biological turn in Popper's thinking which was present in 1935 and flowered during the 1960s.

INTRODUCTION

Why does Karl Popper matter?

Karl Popper is best known for the falsifiability criterion of science which specifies that a system is only to be regarded as empirical or scientific if it is capable of being tested (refuted or falsified) by experience. That is only the tip of the iceberg of his thinking because he made many important contributions to the philosophy of science and in several other fields including political philosophy, the theory of knowledge, rationality, and the history of ideas. The main lines of his work should be common knowledge and they can be sketched in two nutshells and some themes.

Popper in two nutshells

Popper explained to Mark Notturno that many of his ideas could be capsulated in two nutshells (Notturno, forthcoming).

First, the statement of critical rationalism in the form "I may be wrong and you may be right, and by an effort, we may get nearer to the truth".

Second, the tetradic problem-solving schema.

$$P_1{\rightarrow}TT{\rightarrow}EE{\rightarrow}P_2,$$

Popper proposed this schema for all kinds of problem solving, from the amoeba to Einstein, so it can function as a method of scientific enquiry and indeed the method of all rational discussion. (1) We start with a problem. (2) We advance, *TTs,* tentative theories to solve the problem. (3) Critical appraisal, including tests, to eliminate errors. (4) A new problem or problems appear. This schema can be generalized across the full range of problem-solving activities, including the evolution of life on earth.

Themes

1. Criticism has a vital and liberating function.

2. All our knowledge is conjectural, even our best scientific knowledge.

3. There is an important domain of objective knowledge in addition to the domain of subjective knowledge and beliefs.

4. Recognize the function of written and unwritten social conventions which function as the "rules of the game" of social life, including the methods of science.

5. Reject "essentialism", that is the extended analysis of the "essential" meaning of words or concepts.

6. Appreciate the function of philosophical, abstract or metaphysical ideas which provide the framework of our thinking, including the "metaphysical research programs" which guide the work of scientists.

7. Explore the evolutionary approach. Take Darwin seriously with all the implications of the trial and error process of problem solving that can be observed in the behaviour of living things from the amoeba to Einstein.

Not all those themes are unique to Popper but they provide an access to understanding the contribution that he made in all of the wide range of issues that he addressed.

Non-justificationism, a third nutshell?

The first three themes combine to generate an alternative program in the philosophy of knowledge and the task of philosophy.

The primary concern of the traditional theory of knowledge was the quest for justified true beliefs. Debates raged over the rival authorities; chiefly between the rationalists or intellectualists who found justification by some form of intuition or insight and the empiricists who looked to the evidence of the senses to provide an authority for genuine knowledge. Both sides wanted justification in some foundational or authoritative sense. Identification of appropriately justified true beliefs would mark the terminus of inquiry.

As Hayek pointed out, the most powerful ideas at any time are those which are held in common by rival parties in a dispute.

> The discussions of every age are filled with the issues on which its leading schools of thought differ. But the general intellectual atmosphere of the time is always determined by the views on which the opposing schools agree. They become the unspoken presuppositions of all thought, and common and unquestioned accepted foundations on which all discussion proceeds. (Hayek, 1979, 367)

In contrast, Popper turned from the mainstream concern with justification to use criticism as the central activity in pursuit of knowledge. This program can be summed up in the nutshell of "non-justificationism". Such is the power of justificationism in the philosophical trade that Popper's position is not considered in most of the books on the shelves devoted to the theory of knowledge in university libraries

See page 167 for more on non-justificationism and critical rationalism. William W. Bartley wrote a great deal to explain the implications of the change of direction from the pursuit of confirmation and justification to criticism and non-justificationism (see the bibliography).

CHAPTER ONE

POPPER'S PROGRESS

Popper's contribution has to be understood against the background of the ideas which dominated Anglo-Saxon philosophy in the early 20th century under the influence of Bertrand Russell, Ernst Mach and Ludwig Wittgenstein. This history has receded from sight among students who came to the party after the "philosophy of science" wars of the 1960s and '70s when Kuhn, Lakatos, Feyerabend and others became key players.

The positivists

The philosophy of science was institutionalised and professionalised in the 1930s when it became an official movement driven by the logical positivists on the Continent and later the logical empiricists in the US. The Vienna Circle of logical positivists gathered around Professor Moritz Schlick (1882-1936), Rudolph Carnap (1891-1970) and Otto Neurath (1883-1945). Their spiritual predecessor was Ernst Mach (1838-1916), a philosopher-physicist in the strong empiricist tradition of David Hume whose mission was to purge science of metaphysics and place it on the firm "positive" foundations of sensory perceptions (especially vision, "seeing is believing"). Few philosophers have had such a deep and wide-ranging influence. Mach virtually became the official philosopher of Viennese progressivism through his influence in psychology, physics (the young Einstein), literature (Robert Musil), and painting (the Impressionists).

The members of the Circle pursued Mach's positivism, inspired by Russell's attempt to reduce mathematics to logic and Wittgenstein's attack on metaphysics. They pursued a "war on metaphysics" using the strict "verificationist" definition of meaning: statements should be regarded as literally meaningless if they could not be confirmed or verified by evidence. The propositions of logic and mathematics were exempt from the requirement for verification on the understanding that they are true by definition and they do not pretend to convey information about the world.

The positive part of their program was to demonstrate how science could be firmly based on the foundations of experience. This called for a satisfactory explanation for the success of the "inductive" methods of science, and a solution to the problem of induction That is, how do we know that general laws are true (all ravens are black, all planets move in ellipses) when we have not observed *all* the ravens or planets in the universe.

Enter Popper

Popper was born in Vienna in 1902 and died in England in 1994. The third child of a prominent liberal lawyer with scholarly interests, he dropped out of school in 1918 and attended university lectures in topics that interested him, especially mathematics and physics. The university was an easy walk from the family apartment in the same building with the rooms of his father's legal practice in the heart of the old city. Also in walking distance were the main Catholic Cathedral, the City Synagogue, the Parliament Building, the Opera House, several major museums and art galleries and Cafe Central. Another "sacred site" that loomed large in his life was the Volksgarten, a public park where in 1935 Alfred Tarski gave him a private lecture on the semantic conception of truth.

The young Popper engaged in radical politics and voluntary social work including a spell with Alfred Adler's welfare project in the slums. Inspired by Tolstoy's views on the dignity of manual work he apprenticed himself to a cabinet maker in 1924. He contemplated a career in music but instead joined the teacher-training course established in the University to support the Austrian school reforms that were under way at the time (he matriculated in 1922). He qualified as a primary school teacher in 1925 and then studied for a doctorate in psychology which he obtained in 1928 followed by a diploma in 1929 to teach mathematics and science in lower secondary schools. He wrote two theses, one on habit formation in children and the other on axiomatic systems of geometry. Karl Buhler was probably his most important teacher because he supervised Popper's doctoral studies and introduced him to the important line of thought on learning and language that was initiated by Selz and Kulpe.

On the way Popper studied philosophy, mathematics and science, with informal assistance from some established philosophers, notably Heinrich Gomperez and Julius Kraft. He courted and married a physical education teacher Josephine Henninger, "Hennie", who became his tireless co-worker until she died in 1985. In the late 1920s he seriously engaged with the twin problems of induction and demarcation and commenced his long argument with the positivists and the logical empiricists.

A time of crisis

Austria was in crisis during the 1930s, especially when Hitler came to power in Germany in 1933. People such as Popper and Ludwig von Mises who read *Mein Kampf* and took it seriously saw disaster coming for Austria and the Jews. On the intellectual front it was a time of crisis in philosophy and physics. The crisis in philosophy was the failure to provide a justification for the logic of induction which was supposed to be the distinctive feature of science. Bertrand Russell used a striking turn of phrase to describe this failure as the "skeleton in the cupboard" of rationalism. He meant that science is supposed to a highly rational enterprise but if the philosophical criticisms of the inductive method cannot be answered, then the credibility of science could suffer and respect for rationality itself would be at risk.

Popper produced his first book *Logik der Forschung* (The Logic of Research) in 1935 and it appeared in English as *The Logic of Scientific*

Discovery in 1959. In the Preface to the English edition Popper suggested that there is no method peculiar to philosophy, that both science and philosophy should use what he called "the one method of all *rational discussion* ... that of stating one's problem clearly and of examining its various proposed solutions *critically*." (Popper 1972, 16). He italicized the words rational discussion and critically to emphasise that he equated the rational attitude and the critical attitude. He also commended a historical approach to find out what other people have contributed to the problem of interest. "If we ignore what other people are thinking, or have thought in the past, then rational discussion must come to an end." (*ibid*,16).

The Logic of Scientific Discovery is one of the great "game changing" books of the 20th century because it showed how scientists could operate without making use of inductive logic – the logic of proceeding from individual observations to natural laws. That eliminated the "skeleton in the cupboard of rationality" and it also provided philosophical support for Einstein's approach and his revolutionary program in physics. In particular Popper supported what he labelled deductivism, that is, the deductive testing of theories in a struggle for survival. "Its aim is not to save the lives of untenable systems but, on the contrary, to select the one which is by comparison the fittest, by exposing them all to the fiercest struggle for survival." (Popper 1972, 42). That is an alternative to the inductive method which essentially calls for collecting data to generate theories and then collecting more data to support or confirm them.

He provided an alternative program to eliminate the "skeleton in the cupboard of rationalism" by explaining how scientists can proceed without depending on the "logic" of induction. He replaced the focus on the justification of beliefs with the process of forming critical preferences among competing theories based on their problem-solving capacity and their ability to survive criticism, including tests.

Positive reception in some quarters

Hacohen's *Karl Popper: The Formative Years 1902-1945* (2000) provides an account of the way *Logik der Forschung* was received when it was hot off the press. It created a stir in Vienna and beyond, and it was widely reviewed for a specialized book on scientific philosophy.

The Austrian economists Morgenstern, Harbeler and Hayek read it very soon after publication and were favourably impressed. Popper sent a copy to Einstein by a circuitous route. He was a lifelong friend of the pianist Rudolf Serkin, who passed the book on to his mother-in-law Frida Busch, wife of the violinist Adolf Busch, who was a friend of Einstein. The book travelled with a note from Frida Busch that the young author did not have an academic position and could use any help that Einstein might offer. Einstein replied warmly, endorsing the philosophy on all the essential points, and he asked what he could do to help. Popper was advised to mention his need for a fellowship but he was overwhelmed and he refused to ask for any assistance from the great man.

Springer printed 860 copies and the 13.50 RM price was equivalent to two to three days work for a schoolteacher like Popper at the time. The sales figures were 200 by July 1935, 415 by October 1937 and 449 by August 1939. The publishers needed to sell 440 copies to break even. The remaining stock came to grief in an Allied bombardment late in the war.

While Popper's ideas never became popular among philosophers he is one of very few philosophers who is appreciated by scientists. That applies to scientists at the top of the tree (Einstein, Medawar, Eccles, and Monod) and also to the humble soil scientists whom he encountered in adult education courses in New Zealand.

The poverty of historicism (historical determinism)

As a man of the moderate left Popper was alarmed at the failure of the socialists to prevent the rise of fascism. Some Marxists managed to convince themselves that this was inevitable, and so could not be resisted. Others claimed that fascism was the last gasp of capitalism and should be allowed to run its course.

Popper escaped the fate of 16 of his relatives by moving to Canterbury College in Christchurch, New Zealand, in 1937. Austria became a part of Germany in 1938 and when the war started Popper was technically an "enemy alien" so he was not allowed to participate in the war effort in uniform. Writing *The Poverty of Historicism* and *The Open Society and Its Enemies* became his war work when Hitler invaded Austria in 1938.

Popper aimed to refute the major arguments which propped up the myth of historical inevitability, sometimes called "the locomotive theory" of history, and also the myth of the chosen people which animated both the Marxists and the Nazis. These are possibly the most dangerous and damaging myths of modern times and the rise of radical Islam has made them topical again. *The Poverty of Historicism* is a neglected classic because it was overshadowed by *The Open Society and Its Enemies* which was published in 1945 while *The Poverty* first appeared in a series of three journal articles in 1944/45 and did not appear in book form until 1957. One of his signature ideas in the book is the approach to social reform that he called "piecemeal social engineering", that is, to proceed in stages with monitoring at each stage to identify unexpected problems and unwanted consequences of the reforms. He also called for a study of institutions as the vital framework of human action, especially to explain scientific and industrial progress.

He wanted to see a body of practical knowledge to enable social reforms to deliver peace, freedom and prosperity in the way that the natural sciences and technology increase the productive capacity of the earth. David Miller has suggested in personal communication that this is very much an Enlightenment dream because science does not really advance technology directly. Indeed Popper's concern in *The Poverty of Historicism* was social technology even more than social science. Still the over-riding point was to be modest and rational (critical) because the kind of piecemeal reforms that he advocated would be subject to abuse, like science and technology, but not as much as grand schemes driven by dictators or "philosopher kings" who believe that "history (or God) is on our side".

A window of opportunity

During the 1930s three men worked on the same problems in the social sciences and they came up with practically the same framework for analysis. Talcott Parsons returned to the US after postgraduate studies in London and Heidelberg to write *The Structure of Social Action* (1937). Ludwig von Mises worked for the Austrian government during the day and in the evenings he worked on "The Fundamental Problems of Political Economy". *Human Action*, his masterwork, appeared in German in 1940 and in English in 1949. Not far away in Vienna Karl Popper worked on "The Two Fundamental Problems of The Theory of Knowledge" after teaching science and mathematics in school. (It seems that both von Mises and Popper were fundamentalists☺).

All three offered a framework for the study of economics and the other social sciences which could have:

- Maintained sociology and economics as an integrated discipline.

- Sponsored partnerships between economists and students of all social institutions - law, politics, literature, religion and cultural studies at large.

- Ensured that "high theory" and empirical studies informed, enriched and corrected each other.

- Contributed to good public policy, especially by monitoring the results of increased regulation and the erosion of "civic virtues".

There was a window of opportunity for these three leading figures in their respective fields, plus their followers, to form a united front across the disciplines of sociology, economics and philosophy to promote the ideas that they shared and to debate the views that they did not share. This did not happen. The published works of Popper and Parsons contain no references to the other parties. No reader of von Mises would be moved to read the work of the other two. So there was no united front across the three disciplines and the defective ideas which all three identified in the 1930s became embedded in the rapidly growing community of academics and researchers after the war.

The Open Society and Its Enemies (1945)

Popper's first book in English was his war effort, a major work which grew out of notes that he made for section 10 on Essentialism in *The Poverty of Historicism. The Open Society and Its Enemies* is a systematic investigation of several powerful ideas which render our traditions of democracy, rationality and tolerance dangerously fragile under the pressure of social and political crises. It is a tract of moral and political philosophy but it has a low profile in university courses at present and in the current literature on moral philosophy and politics.

Popper's critique of Plato and Marx has often described as unfair. It is essential to appreciate that he revered Plato's achievement and he appreciated the contribution of Marx but in each case he identified some of their ideas as dangerous for the cause of freedom. His aim was to eliminate errors, not to denigrate their achievements.

For Popper, moral and political philosophy should be concerned with the formulation and criticism *of the written and unwritten "rules of the game" in social life.* These rules occur in all groups and they may be enforced informally or by due process of law. The question we have to face is not whether we will have rules but whether we will try to improve them by critical discussion and trial and error. This approach cuts through the verbalism that bogs down a lot of discussion of moral and politics because it is constantly in touch with problems of interest and their possible solutions. The issues that can be addressed in this manner range from the sharing of household chores to Constitutional reform and major international agreements. This approach could have evolved out of Wittgenstein's concern with games and forms of life if he or his followers had engaged in a critical and problem-oriented approach to scientific investigation or practical and political issues. *The Open Society and Its Enemies*, first published in 1945, also challenged dominant schools of thought, on the conservative side the admirers of Plato and Aristotle, on the other side the adherents of Hegel and Marx. Popper did not belittle the achievements of Plato, and Marx, indeed he paid them generous compliments while he directed his critical attention on ideas which confuse and divide the friends of freedom, making way for totalitarian regimes in the 20th century and beyond.

Conjectures and Refutations (1963)

During the 1950s Popper translated *Logik der Forschung* and in the process he wrote a lot of new notes, indeed so many that they grew into a separate volume which was intended to appear in 1955, titled *The Postscript to The Logic of Scientific Discovery: After Twenty Years* (from 1935). Publication of *The Postscript* was delayed for two more decades due to problems with Popper's eyes and other projects including the collection of a bundle of essays for *Conjectures and Refutations*.

Despite Popper's intense activity during the 1950s there was little to show outside the academic journals apart from the very small and somewhat enigmatic *The Poverty of Historicism* in 1957 and the very technical *The Logic of Scientific Discovery* in 1959. Neither of those volumes provided a readily accessible introduction to his thought.

Conjectures and Refutations contains 21 papers on a very wide range of topics to consolidate and extend the insights of *The Open Society* and *The Logic of Scientific Discovery*. Chapter 1 "Science: Conjectures and Refutations" was prepared for a 1953 conference on trends and developments in British philosophy. It contains his first account of the evolution of his ideas and a list of thirteen areas of interest that he was exploring at the time. These ranged from probability theories and problems in the formalization of quantum theory to the nature of scientific objectivity in relation to the sociology of science.

Popper's publication program did not work out well for the propagation of his ideas or for his own standing in the profession. *Logik der*

Forschung was practically invisible in the English-speaking world after the war and the Continental diaspora entrenched logical positivism and logical empiricism in the English and North American universities while Popper was relatively isolated in New Zealand from 1937 to the end of 1945. Then during the 1950s various forms of linguistic philosophy became the major rivals to positivism for professional attention among those who were not interested in the so-called Continental schools of thought. Consequently both *The Logic of Scientific Discovery* and *Conjectures and Refutations* were published against the trend of philosophical thinking which was soon flowing with Kuhn's *The Structure of Scientific Revolutions* (1962) because Kuhn provided a much more exciting and accessible alternative to "the establishment" or "the received view" in the philosophy of science.

Objective Knowledge (1972)

In the 1960s Popper produced a series of conference papers on the theme of evolution with a stronger account of objective knowledge than his dismissal of psychologism in *The Logic of Scientific Discovery*. The papers were collected in *Objective Knowledge: An Evolutionary Approach*. They addressed a linked set of problems concerning biological evolution, human consciousness, language and the nature of abstract ideas. Following Buhler, Popper he argued that the distinctive features of human society and culture resulted from our use of language for description and argument, functions that cannot be reduced to the expressive and signalling functions of language.

He revived an approach to knowledge called evolutionary epistemology which was popular in the nineteenth century but lapsed in the twentieth due to the obsession with physics in the philosophy of science. Evolutionary epistemology applies Darwin's principle of natural selection to scientific theories and to other forms of knowledge. It is concerned with problem-solving and error-elimination under various forms of selective pressure.

The central motif of Popper's evolutionary epistemology is the four-step problem-solving schema, noted before as the "second nutshell".

$$P \dashrightarrow TS \dashrightarrow EE \dashrightarrow P$$

The starting point is a problem, which evokes tentative solutions. These are subjected to the process of error elimination by way of critical discussion and experimental testing. In the course of these activities new problems emerge. This schema brings out the importance of recognizing problems and working on them because a problem functions as an ecological niche to be colonised by tentative solutions. Thus a problem should be seen as an opportunity and problems are the growing points of science. This functions as a theory of discovery, based on the creative function of criticism. Problems can be said to create "habitats" where new ideas grow and criticism has two functions, which are about equally valuable: (a) to eliminate error and (b) is to generate new problem situations to function as new "habitats" which provide opportunities for innovation. *Thus Popper's theory brings out both the error elimination and the creative function of criticism, and we need to maximise the free play of criticism to get the best out of both functions.*

The Schilpp volume, *Unended Quest* and *The Self and Its Brain*

In 1974 came the long-awaited Popper volume in the Library of Living Philosophers series, edited by P. A. Schilpp. The books in this series provide an intellectual autobiography of the subject, followed by a collection of descriptive and critical essays, then replies by the philosopher.

An unintended benefit of the Schilpp volume came about when William W. Bartley published a series of review essays (Bartley, 1976, 1978, 1980). This revived his appreciation of Popper's work, collaboration resumed and Bartley completed the task of preparing the Postscript.

The Self and its Brain came from another collaborative project with Popper's friend from New Zealand, the Nobel Prizewinning neuroscientist John Eccles. The book has three parts, first Popper's

20

review of philosophical theories of the body-mind relationship, then an account from Eccles of the current state of knowledge of the anatomy and physiology of the brain, and thirdly the transcripts of several long conversations between the two authors. The work is an extended argument for interactionism (signalled by the subtitle of the book) and this was very much out of step with the philosophical orthodoxy. The book is often accused of being dualist, maybe even Cartesian but that is not an accurate account because it is pluralist, and Popper did not accept anything like a mental substance.

The Postscript to The Logic of Scientific Discovery

The Postscript to The Logic of Scientific Discovery finally emerged from Bartley's editorial hands in three volumes during 1982 and 1983. The long delay in publication is unfortunate because the important idea of metaphysical research programs appeared during the 1970s in a very different form created by Imre Lakatos. Early forms of the manuscript circulated among Popper's colleagues, including Lakatos, who took up the idea of research programs and put forth a complicated "methodology of scientific research programs" (MSRP). This aroused intense interest and the competition between the MSRP and Kuhn's theory of paradigms caused a great deal of confusion and misplaced effort which might have been avoided if *The Postscript* had appeared earlier.

The three volumes of *The Postscript* are *Realism and the Aim of Science* (Volume 1), *The Open Universe: An Argument for Indeterminism* (Volume 2) and *Quantum Theory and the Schism in Physics* (Volume 3). They contribute to Popper's long campaign in support of realism, indeterminism and objectivism which in turn support human freedom, creativity and rationality.

The author's 1982 Introduction to *Realism and the Aim of Science* responds briefly to a claim that T. S. Kuhn provided a refutation or even a serious criticism of Popper's ideas. After the launch of *The Structure of Scientific Revolutions* Kuhn retracted most of his radical views and adopted a more realistic position, so Popper could write in *Realism and the Aim of Science* "On the question of the significance of falsification for the history of science, Kuhn's and my views coincide almost completely." (xxxi).

Kuhn himself wrote:

> Even in the developed sciences, there is an essential role for Sir Karl's methodology. It is the strategy appropriate to those occasions when something goes wrong with normal science, when the discipline encounters crisis. (Kuhn, 1970, 247)

A "crisis" is a situation where generally accepted theories are challenged, something that can happen at any time when scientists are alert, which is much more often than proponents of normal science realize as Firestein explained in *Ignorance: How it Drives Science*.

It seems that by the 1980s most philosophers had lost interest in Popper and they did not notice the rejoinder to Kuhn at the start of *Realism and the Aim of Science* or the theory of metaphysical research programs in *Quantum Theory and the Schism in Physics*.

Realism and the Aim of Science has two parts, the first treats inductivism, and the way it is underpinned by subjectivism and idealism (the world is my dream). The second attacks the subjective interpretation of the probability calculus.

Popper critically reviewed four aspects of inductivism; the logical, methodological, epistemological and metaphysical. In the course of that survey he explained how his theory of falsifiability responded to some central issues in epistemology and he restated the significance of falsifiability in demarcating scientific, non-scientific, pseudoscientific and metaphysical theories from each other. He placed his ideas in the context of modern empiricism by engaging with the positions of Berkeley, Hume, Kant, Russell and Mach, especially by rejecting the quest for justification of beliefs. He favourably noted Bartley's commentary on "non-justificationism" and the way that Bartley placed this in the forefront of his exegesis of Popper's ideas (Bartley 1976, 1980, 1984).

The second part of *Realism* demonstrates a significant development of his ideas about probability from The Logic of Scientific Discovery. He attacked the subjective interpretation of the probability calculus and the belief that probability measures a subjective degree of ignorance. In *The Logic of Scientific Discovery* he pursued his objective interpretation of the probability calculus using the frequency interpretation but in *Realism* he rejected the frequency interpretation and instead proposed his own propensity interpretation. This evolved from a theory of probability to become a whole cosmology - a world of propensities!

In his editor's foreword Bartley pointed out the deep connection between the arguments in the first and second volumes "in their mutual concern with the freedom, creativity and rationality of man". The first volume, *Realism and the Aim of Science*, explained how non-justificationism (the conjectural theme) supports rationality and refutes subjectivist and sceptical claims about the logical limits of criticism (hence the limits to rationality). The treatment of determinism in the second, *The Open Universe*, claimed that we are limited in our ability to anticipate the future growth of human knowledge but this limitation does not undermine our rationality. If this limit did not exist then our exchange of arguments about our actions and policies would be meaningless (because what will be, will be, regardless of our arguments).

> Popper thus argues that human reason is unlimited with regard to criticism yet limited with regard to its powers of prediction; and shows that both the lack of limitation and the limitation are, in their respective places, necessary for human rationality to exist at al.l (*Realism and the Aim of Science*, xv)

The Open Universe drew a distinction between two kinds of determinism, the scientific and the metaphysical. Contrary to those who make the case for indeterminism on the basis of modern physics, Popper argued that classical physics need not presuppose or imply determinism any more than quantum physics does. The systematic nature of his thinking comes through in the connection that can be traced between subjective interpretations of probability and the way that metaphysical determinism persists in quantum physics even while the physicist may resist the scientific form of determinism.

The four chapters are "Kinds of Determinism", "'Scientific' Determinism", "The Case for Indeterminism" and "Metaphysical Issues". The chapter on metaphysical issues describes the theory of propensities as a gain for science. An Afterword and two especially interesting and important addenda are attached. "Indeterminism is not enough: An afterword" originally appeared in the monthly magazine *Encounter* in April 1973.

The first addendum, "Scientific reduction and the essential incompleteness of all science" is a rejoinder to all the over-optimistic scientists who have ever proclaimed that the "end of the road" is near, that science (usually physics) is on the verge of delivering The Final Theory Of Everything. He pointed out that Godel's incompleteness theorem of arithmetic provides a formal demolition of the "end of the road" aspiration, although he regarded that as "heavy argument against a comparatively weak position". Popper's world (of propensities) is a world of emergent evolution, emergent novelty, where problems may be solved but in the process deeper problems appear.

The theme of the third volume of the *Postscript* is the way that the Copenhagen interpretation of quantum physics has been influenced by unstated and uncriticised metaphysical assumptions, especially determinism, subjectivism and instrumentalism. The followers of the Copenhagen "school" are scientific indeterminists but Popper argued that there is a metaphysical form of determinism that they had not eliminated from their thinking.

There are four chapters after a 1982 Preface and an Introduction. The Preface makes a case for a realistic and commonsense interpretation of quantum theory to overcome the crisis in physics which Popper attributed to two things, the intrusion of subjectivism and the "end of the road" idea that quantum theory has reached the complete and final truth. In the Introduction he argues for an interpretation of quantum physics without the observer and he sharply formulated thirteen theses to challenge the Copenhagen interpretation of the observer as an integral part of every observed system.

In Chapter I, "Understanding Quantum Theory and its Interpretations" Popper updated his ideas from the formulations in The Logic of Scientific Discovery. He still maintained that the problem of interpreting quantum theory is bound up with the interpretation of probability theory, and he argued that the theory of propensities that he described in the first and second volumes of *The Postscript* should be applied to the interpretation of quantum theory, thus resolving the difficulties that arise in the Copenhagen interpretation.

Chapter II "The Objectivity of Quantum Theory" returned to the issue of the observer in the system and confronted the doctrine that experiments have to be interpreted with the observer, and especially the consciousness of the observer, as one of the variables. The discussion includes the nature of quantum jumps and the existence or non-existence of particles.

Chapter III attempts a resolution of the paradoxes of quantum theory, using the propensity interpretation of probability, applied to (1) the indeterminacy relations, (2) the experiment of Einstein, Podolsky and Rosen, and (3) the two-slit experiment.

The long fourth chapter is the Metaphysical Epilogue. This covers a lot of ground, starting with a brief statement of the theory of metaphysical research programs (below). He then ran through a series of ten research programs. First the block universe of Parmenides, then several stages including Aristotle's essentialism and potentialism to the clockwork theory and finally the statistical interpretation of quantum theory. After a discussion of schisms, programs and metaphysical dreams he went on to indeterminism and the reduction of the wave packet and a model of a universe of propensities to account for the leading features of all the ten programs that he sketched previously. After touching on some open problems he concluded with some comments on the role of metaphysical systems – to create a unified picture of the world - and the possibility of a demarcation within metaphysics, between good and bad systems.

Metaphysical research programs (MRPs)

Popper's theory of MRPs flows from his theory that we should look at the history of a subject, and its current status, in terms of its problem situations. He saw problem situations arising in three ways. First, the discovery of an inconsistency within the ruling theory. Second, a robust (credible or repeatable) experimental result that is not consistent with the theory. Third is the relation between the theory and what may be called the "metaphysical research programme".

The research program is a vital part of what Polanyi called "tacit knowledge", the seldom stated but all-important framework of thought, Kuhns, "paradigm" which inculcates "railway lines of thought" as scientists proceed through their education and training. Liam Hudson provided a fascinating and revealing account of that process at work in psychologists in Britain during the 1950s (Hudson, 1964).

> By raising the problems of explanation which the theory is designed to solve, the metaphysical research programme makes it possible to judge the success of the theory as an explanation. On the other hand, the critical discussion of the theory and its results may lead to a change in the research programme (usually an unconscious change, as the programme is often held unconsciously, and taken for granted), or to its replacement by another programme. These programmes are only occasionally discussed as such: more often, they are implicit in the theories and in the attitudes and judgements of the scientists.
>
> I call these research programmes "metaphysical" also because they result from general views of the structure of the world and, at the same time, from general views of the problem situation in physical cosmology. I call them "research programmes" because they

incorporate, together with a view of what the most pressing problems are, a general idea of what a satisfactory solution of these problems would look like. (Popper, 1982, 161)

After *The Postscript*

The Postscript was the last major book which Popper produced but several volumes of previously unpublished articles, interviews and correspondence were still to come, some of them after he died in 1994.

1990. *A World of Propensities*.

1992. *In Search of a Better World: Lectures and Essays from Thirty Years*.

1994. *Knowledge and the Body-Mind Problem: In Defence of Interactionism*, edited by M. A. Notturno.

1994. *The Myth of the Framework: In Defence of Science and Rationality*, edited by M. A. Notturno.

1998. *The World of Parmenides: Essays on the Presocratic Enlightenment*, edited by A. F. Petersen.

1999. *All Life is Problem-Solving*.

2008. *The Two Fundamental Problems in the Theory of Knowledge* (the precursor of The Logic of Scientific Discovery) edited by Troels Eggers Hansen.

2008. *After the Open Society: Selected Social and Political Writing*, edited by Jeremy Shearmur and Piers Norris Turner.

CHAPTER TWO

THE POPPER LEGEND

The Legend in this context is the idea that Popper can be aggregated with the positivists and logical empiricists and then ignored because that program was upstaged in progressive circles by Kuhn, Lakatos and Feyerabend. Later Philip Kitcher used the label "Legend" to refer to the time when the logical empiricists hoped to explain the success of science by a logical account of the scientific method (Kitcher, 1993, Chapter 1). The Popper Legend survived because the logical empiricists and others did not take the central Popperian themes seriously enough to accept that his approach represented a helpful and progressive alternative to logical empiricism. Popper was not really a party to the Legend described by Kitcher but readers focussed on the narrowest possible interpretation of his contribution which was called "falsificationism" as though the only difference between the two programs was "falsificationism" versus verificationism. Popper rejected two major elements of the positivist/empiricist program; (1) the quest for a criterion of meaning or "cognitive significance" and (2) the justification of beliefs by way of inductive probabilities. Consequently the protagonists of that program were not prepared to take seriously his alternative approach and instead they insisted that he exaggerated their differences and even misunderstood Carnap's work on probability and confirmation theory.

As noted in Popper's Progress (above) Hacohen wrote an account of the early reception of *Logik der Forschung.* Carnap was very impressed and "Polish logicians Kotarbinski and Tarski thought it extraordinary, and young philosophers Ayer, Hempel and Nagel were in awe." (Hacohen, 2000, 276). On the other hand, several circle members, Frank, Neurath, and Schlick were critical, "even outraged", as were the physicists in Heisenberg's group. Carnap was supportive but he wrote to Popper to complain that he had exaggerated his differences with the Circle. This was a theme that persisted among Circle supporters and then the logical empiricists for the rest of their lives.

Carnap eventually accepted the idea of falsifiability (testability) but he used it as *a criterion of meaning* and this added weight to the Popper Legend because it reinforced the perception that Popper was concerned with *meaning*, like the positivists. In private, Schlick, the leader of the movement, lectured Popper about his wilful attacks on positivism and indicated that he had irreparably damaged his relations with the Circle.

Popper described what he called the "Popper Legend" in his reply to critics in *The Philosophy of Karl Popper* in the Library of Living Philosophers series. According to the legend Popper was a positivist, maybe even a member of the Vienna Circle, and he proposed falsifiability as the criterion of meaning instead of the verification principle to banish metaphysics from polite conversations.

Ayer's book *Language, Truth and Logic* (1936) was probably the first statement of the Legend in English and for some time it was the standard text on the new philosophy of science for English-speaking people. His limpid prose, inspired, like Popper, by Bertrand Russell, ensured that his works were widely read by people who were not professional philosophers. Ayer was friendly and helpful with Popper in England in 1936 but he did not clarify the true situation regarding Popper's work even when the book was reprinted several times.

Carnap and Hempel sponsored the legend they became the leaders of the positivist-empiricist movement in the United States and in their lifelong quest for some criterion of "cognitive meaningfulness" they never modified the message that Popper shared their concerns and perversely exaggerated the distance between them.

The perception of Popper's work could have changed when *The Logic of Scientific Discovery* appeared in English in 1959 but it was expensive, like the *Logik* and did not circulate widely before Kuhn's *The Structure of Scientific Revolutions* became the best-known critique of the positivists and logical empiricists.

CHAPTER THREE

THE LOGIC OF SCIENTIFIC DISCOVERY

Why *The Logic of Scientific Discovery* matters

Karl Popper's *The Logic of Scientific Discovery* is one of the great "game changing" books of the 20th century. Originally published in 1934 (imprint 1935) as *Logik der Forschung* (The Logic of Scientific Investigation) it provided an alternative program to logical positivism and empiricism in the philosophy of science and in epistemology at large.

Popper: out of step

Popper's work is so out of step with the profession of philosophers these days that a special effort may be required to understand why so many practicing scientists have appreciated it —both scientists at the top of the tree and also the humble soil scientists who Popper lectured in adult education classes in New Zealand. The Nobel Prize winners Albert Einstein, Peter Medawar, John Eccles and Jacques Monod saluted his work. Medawar described Popper as possibly the greatest philosopher of science, and Monod commenced his introduction to the French translation of *The Logic of Scientific Discovery* with the words "This great and noble book".

The book introduced several of the themes that represent Popper's major contributions, among them the inherently conjectural nature of scientific knowledge, objectivism (paying attention to statements and theories rather than sense impressions and beliefs), and recognition of the role of methodological conventions or "rules of the game" in science.

Not a good book for beginners

The Logic of Scientific Discovery is a difficult book for beginners. It was written for a time of philosophical crisis and it is necessary to understand the state of play in philosophy and science at that time, something which may have slipped the attention of students who commenced their studies during the philosophy of science wars of the 1960s and afterwards. Beginners may thus feel "lost" due to the lack of familiar "landmarks," such as the demand for justification or confirmation. Identifying the themes which were spelled out in the Introduction will help students find their way and explore what happens when old problems are reformulated and addressed in new ways.

One aspect of the book may distract attention from the major issues, this is the amount of "fine print" in the language used to formulate its arguments and especially the nature of "the empirical basis," which obsessed the positivists due to their desire to ground all knowledge on sense perception and sensations. There a lot of technical detail in the chapters on degrees of testability, simplicity, probability and physics. The good news is that most of the essential ideas can be gleaned from 60 pages in Part I and 30 pages in the chapter on corroboration. That is less than 100 pages of a book which ran over 280 pages in the first version, boosted by 150 pages of new appendices and extra notes in the English edition.

Background

As explained in "Popper's Progress" his contribution has to be understood against the background of the ideas that dominated Anglo-Saxon philosophy in the early 20th century under the influence of Ernst Mach, Bertrand Russell, Ludwig Wittgenstein and the logical positivists, including the Vienna Circle.

The members of the Circle pursued Mach's positivism, inspired by Russell's attempt to reduce mathematics to logic and Wittgenstein's attack on metaphysics. The war on metaphysics was pursued using the strict "verificationist" definition of meaning which decreed that statements should be regarded as literally meaningless if they could not be confirmed or verified by empirical evidence. The positive part of the positivist program was to demonstrate how science could be firmly based on the foundations of experience. This called for a satisfactory logical account of the inductive methods of science, and a solution to the problem of induction itself. That is the problem of confirming universal statements (such as 'all planets move in ellipses') while we can never observe all the planets in the galaxy.

Popper's progress

Readers will recall that Popper dropped out of school late in 1918 and attended lectures at the University of Vienna as a non-matriculated student. He trained as a science teacher and completed his qualification in 1929 after majoring in psychology and writing two theses, one on habit formation in children and the other on the axioms of the various schools of geometry. He studied philosophy independently with some informal assistance from a number of scholars, including some who were attached to the Vienna Circle. During 1929 he locked onto the twin problems of induction and demarcation and embarked on a lifelong debate with the logical positivists/empiricists. This unfortunately tended to distract attention from other important work that he did after *Logik der Forschung*.

A time of crisis

The crisis in philosophy was the failure to provide a justification for the logic of induction, which was supposed to be the distinctive feature of science. Bertrand Russell described this as the "skeleton in the cupboard" of rationalism. Another looming disaster for the positivists was the failure of the verification criterion to provide a workable demarcation between science and metaphysics. In physics there was the problem of understanding Einstein's challenge to Newton and the tension between Bohr and Einstein on the interpretation of quantum theory.

Logik der Forschung

Logik der Forschung is a savagely edited version of a large manuscript entitled *Die Beiden Grundprobleme der Erkenntnistheories* which was eventually published in German in 1979 and in English in 2009 under the title *The Two Fundamental Problems of the Theory of Knowledge*.

In his Preface to the first edition of *The Logic of Scientific Discovery* Popper suggested that there is no method peculiar to philosophy, that both science and philosophy should use the method of rational or critical analysis "of stating one's problem clearly and of examining its various proposed solutions critically". He also commended a version of the historical method to find out what other people have contributed to the problem of interest. "If we ignore what other people are thinking, or have thought in the past, then rational discussion must come to an end."

The book as it exists today consists of two parts, followed by two sets of appendices, one from 1935 and a new set added while the book was being translated in the 1950s. The new footnotes and appendices grew into another book, *The Postscript to The Logic of Scientific Discovery*, which eventually appeared in three volumes in the 1980s.

CONTENTS

PREFACE

INTRODUCTION

PART I: INTRODUCTION TO THE LOGIC OF SCIENCE
Chapter 1. A Survey of Some Fundamental Problems
Chapter 2. On the Problem of a Theory of Scientific Method
PART II: SOME STRUCTURAL COMPONENTS OF A THEORY OF EXPERIENCE
Chapter 3. Theories
Chapter 4. Falsifiability
Chapter 5. The Problem of the Empirical Basis

PART I

Introduction to the Logic of Science

Chapter I. A Survey of Some Fundamental Problems

Popper confronted the view that the distinctive feature of empirical science is the use of induction to derive general theories from the repeated observation of individual facts and to confirm or justify those theories with further observations.

Isaac Newton's *Principia* was supposed to represent the crowning glory of induction. Newton said that he used the inductive method, and he claimed that there was no guesswork, no hypothesis; "I feign no hypotheses." A generation or so later David Hume cast doubt on the logic of induction by showing that the conclusion of an inductive argument could be false even if all of its premises were true—and that our general knowledge of matters of fact was based upon nothing more than custom and habit. This, Kant tells us, is what awakened him from his "dogmatic slumbers" and led him to attempt to explain the miracle of science, namely, how science could produce theories which are strictly universal, necessarily true, and apodictically certain (such as Newtonian mechanics and Euclidean geometry), even though the inductive arguments, which are supposed to justify them, are logically invalid.

The unsolved problem of induction haunted the logical positivists and empiricists in general throughout the 20th century.

The problem of induction

Popper rejected induction, both as a method of discovery and as a method of justification, and he upheld deduction as the logic of science. "The theory to be developed in the following pages stands directly opposed to all attempts to operate with the ideas of inductive logic. It might be described as the theory of the *deductive method of testing*." (30).

He called this view "deductivism", in contrast with "inductivism", and he made a distinction between the psychology of knowledge and the logic of knowledge. The former is concerned with sensations and facts. The latter is concerned only with logical relations. This distinction is important in Popper's approach because one of the supports for the so-called "inductive logic" of science is the almost universal assumption in traditional epistemology that knowledge is a matter of subjective belief (psychology). He wanted to pursue to scientific knowledge as a body of theories which can be examined without reference to psychology and some years later he developed a more articulated theory of objective knowledge.

Elimination of psychologism

Maintaining his anti-psychological stance, Popper refused to be drawn into discussion about the act of conceiving or inventing or discovering a theory because he did not see how it could be subjected to logical analysis. For Popper the logic of scientific investigation is the logic of deductive testing and the methods that can be used for that purpose. He insisted that scientific theories need to be subjected to systematic tests (and to pass at least some of them) if they are to be taken seriously. He acknowledged that the process of conceiving a new idea could be a very interesting topic for psychologists and historians, but he did not see how studies in those fields can help to assess the validity of a theory.

Deductive testing of theories

Popper identified four methods of deductive testing.

1. Checking for internal consistency (whether or not a theory is self-contradictory).

2. Checking the logical form to see if it is empirical (scientific) or tautological.

3. Comparison with other theories to see if it is potentially an advance.

4. Empirical tests.

The purpose of this last kind of test is to find out how far the new consequences of the theory stand up to the demands of practice…"Nothing resembling inductive logic appears in the procedure here outlined…I never assume that by force of 'verified' conclusions, theories can be established as 'true', or even as merely 'probable'." (33).

The problem of demarcation

The problem of demarcation is the problem of finding a criterion to distinguish between the empirical sciences and a variety of non-empirical theories including mathematics, logic, 'metaphysical' systems, moral and political principles, conventions of scientific method, and, incidentally, nonsense. On Popper's account, the problem of demarcation was forced upon Kant when he encountered Hume's classical critique of induction and so it became arguably the central problem in the theory of knowledge.

Popper saw the problems of demarcation and induction as the source of nearly all the other problems of the theory of knowledge. He saw the problem of demarcation as the more fundamental of the two, because empiricists in general and the positivists in particular thought that induction was the method of science.

At this point Popper made a significant departure from the approaches that are usually used to decide these matters. Instead of employing logical analysis or observing the way scientists work, Popper talked about the "rules of the game" of science and its "methodological conventions." This approach is closely related to his rejection of certainty as an aim of science. He thus introduced the theme of conjectural knowledge as a permanent feature of scientific theories instead of a transient situation or "bug" in a theory that will be superseded by further investigation and "confirmation". It is also closely related to his perception of the social nature of science which was little-noticed prior to Jarvie's book *The Republic of Science* (2001).

Popper's criterion of demarcation is thus a proposal for an agreement or convention. Popper noted that his convention would be rejected by people who think that science can generate a system of "absolutely certain, irrevocably true statements." He suggested that the test for his convention would be to examine its logical consequences, and also to its fertility in solving problems in the theory of knowledge and scientific investigation. Essentially, it would be a test of its practice and practical results.

Experience as a method

In the same way that the conventions for scientific investigation are to be evaluated by their practical value, scientific theories are to evaluated by their capacity to stand up to the test of practice. This means comparing the deductive consequences of theories with observations (the world of experience).

Falsifiability as a criterion of demarcation

The positivists wanted a criterion of demarcation that would conclusively decide whether a statement was verified or falsified (otherwise the statement would be meaningless).

In contrast, for Popper, it must be possible for an empirical scientific system to be refuted by experience. He anticipated some objections that might be raised, and many critics have not noticed that their objections were met in advance. For example he saw the possibility of evading falsification by a number of fairly obvious strategies, such as inventing an ad hoc auxiliary hypothesis, changing a definition, or even refusing to acknowledge problematic data.

To anticipate that possibility Popper clearly stated his move to the "rules of the game" approach, using what he described later in *The Open Society and Its Enemies* as the "language of political proposals or demands". He proposed that the empirical (scientific) method calls for theories to be thoroughly exposed to tests "in every conceivable way". He wrote that the aim is not to save theories but "on the contrary, to select the one which is by comparison the fittest, by exposing them all to the fiercest struggle for survival." (42).

The problem of the 'empirical basis'

The problem of the empirical basis concerns the status of the so-called observation or "basic" statements which we use to test an empirical theory. Popper argued that such statements are not justified by our sense perceptions—this is part of his elimination of psychologism—but they are accepted or rejected on the basis of a free decision. This is treated in more detail in Chapter 5.

Scientific objectivity and subjective conviction

Popper did not wish to be drawn into another round of "interminable discussions" about the words 'objective' and 'subjective' and their burden of contradictory usages. For his purpose objectivity means exposing ideas to public scrutiny so that any interested person can follow the debate and other investigators can repeat the observations and the experiments.

> I hold that scientific theories are never fully justifiable or verifiable, but that they are nevertheless testable. I shall therefore say that the objectivity of scientific statements lies in the fact that they can be inter-subjectively tested. (44)

In practice inter-subjective testing requires some standard procedures and protocols for working scientists, like the detailed description of experimental methods so the work can be repeated by others to ensure that an important result is not a "one off" phenomenon.

Chapter II. On the Problem of a Theory of Scientific Method

It is helpful to recall that Popper was a Professor of Logic *and* Scientific Method, though he insisted that the kind of scientific method that was traditionally sought—a method that assures success — cannot be found. He made a distinction between the purely logical analysis of the relations between statements and the choice of methods, which depends on a choice among proposals for various ways of handling statements. These proposals will flow from the aims that we have adopted for our activities. Since Popper's overall aim was to promote the critical approach to science, his methodological proposals were designed to identify errors and inconsistencies in our existing knowledge, and especially attempts to avoid accepting refutation, falsification, and the possibility that there may be problems in our existing theories. These are the problems which we most need to address to make progress in science.

Why methodological decisions are indispensable

Methodological decisions cannot be avoided because we are constantly faced with problems that cannot be solved by logical analysis alone, such as the situation where a highly successful theory is challenged by adverse evidence (anomalies). At the start of the 20th century Newton's dynamics was in that position and Popper was critical of people who were prepared to hold it dogmatically and demand conclusive disproof. He argued that no conclusive disproof of a theory can ever be produced because observations can be challenged (the apparatus was faulty) or the problem is transient (the theory will be developed to accommodate the discrepancies). "If you insist on strict proof (or strict disproof in the empirical sciences, you will never benefit from experience, and never learn from it how wrong you are." (50).

The naturalistic approach to the theory of method

The naturalistic approach is to look at what scientists actually do, in the hope that this will resolve problems of method. This approach is even more popular today than it was in the 1930s due to the failure of the program of logical analysis and the intractability of the problem of induction, as the positivists/empiricists perceived it. Inductive logic morphed into the quest for numerical probability values to attach to theories as a substitute for their justification while the naturalistic approach has generated a large literature in the sociology and anthropology of science.

Methodological rules as conventions

Popper explained the function of methodological rules as regulative principles or "rules" of the game of science and he suggested two examples.

> (1) The game of science is, in principle, without end. He who decides one day that scientific statements do not call for any further test, and that they can be regarded as finally verified, retires from the game.
>
> (2) Once a hypothesis has been proposed and tested, and has proved its mettle, it may not be allowed to drop out without 'good reason'. A 'good reason' may be, for instance: replacement of the hypothesis by another which is better testable; or the falsification of one of the consequences of the hypothesis. (53-54)

In *The Republic of Science* Jarvie spelled out what he called Popper's "social turn" to take account of the institutions and rules of the game of science. Jarvie compiled a list of 14 rules gleaned from close reading of *The Logic of Scientific Discovery* (Jarvie, 2001, Chapter 2). See the Appendix at the end of this chapter for the list.

PART II

Some Structural Components of a Theory of Experience

Chapter III. Theories

This chapter addresses Causality, Explanation, and the Deduction of Predictions; Strict and Numerical Universality; Universal Concepts and Individual Concepts; Theoretical Systems; Levels of Universality and the Modus Tollens.

Regarding causality and explanation Popper wrote that he did not assert that any event can be causally explained but instead he proposed a methodological rule "that we are not to abandon the search for universal laws and for a coherent theoretical system, nor ever give up our attempts to explain causally any kind of event we can describe" (61) The rule was designed to challenge the view that quantum-level events were inherently beyond causal explanation. Popper described causal explanation as the process of deducing a consequence from a combination of universal laws and the initial conditions at a particular time and place. This later became known as the Nomological-Deductive, or Covering Law, Model of Explanation.

The sections on Strict and Numerical Universality; Universal Concepts and Individual Concepts; and on Strictly Universal and Existential statements are examples of the "fine print" required to take account of the many logical possibilities and implications involved in testing different kinds of statements. These issues arise again in the chapter on Falsifiability.

Moving on to consider axiom systems and the axiomatization of theories, he explained Hilbert's early 20th century project to portray large parts of physical theory in the form of an axiom system, using a minimum of postulates with the rest of the system derived by logic and mathematics. Popper did not regard that project as an end in itself, but rather as a way to explore the impact of changes in one part of the system on other parts, especially the implications of new or revised theories and also falsifications. This involved more heavy duty work on the fine print!

Finally, on the logic of deductive testing and the Modus Tollens he explained how the deductive logic used for explanation (with a general theory in association with initial conditions) is also used to test (refute or falsify) the theory using the classical Modus Tollens form of argument. This is "the mode of argument that denies".

The form of the argument runs as follows:

1. IF P, then Q
2. Not-Q
3. Therefore, Not-P

Here, the P that is refuted consists of an explanatory theory in conjunction with a number of other statements, including ancillary statements of background knowledge and initial conditions. Q is the event or observation predicted by P. If we do not observe Q we infer that the theory is false because the consequence that we have deduced from it is false.

Popper acknowledged that the test involves a set of initial conditions and ancillary hypotheses (theories) and so:

> ...we falsify *the whole system* (the theory as well as the initial conditions) which was required for the deduction of the [observation] statement...Thus it cannot be asserted of any one statement of the system that it is, or is not, specifically upset by the falsification. (76)

It is always this conjunction of statements, and not simply the explanatory theory that we want to test, which is corroborated or refuted by the argument. This does not undermine the logic of investigation as described by Popper, it just means that testing a theory is a complicated process, as explained below.

Chapter IV. Falsifiability

This chapter begins with Popper's rejoinder to conventionalism and proceeds to a fine-grained analysis of the logic of testing. Popper's criticism of so-called Conventionalist Objections could initially be confusing because Popper's own approach to methods is sometimes called "conventionalism" to indicate the importance he attached to conventions (the rules of the game). The conventionalism which Popper criticized was the tendency to protect a ruling theory by making adjustments that do not add content. This practice was prevalent among supporters of Newton in the face of Einstein's challenge. Popper conceded that conventionalism could be self-contained and defensible but he dissented from it because he had a different conception of the aims and purposes of science. Conventionalism is essentially conservative and Popper was in favour of exciting, even revolutionary advances in science. The conventionalist will feel threatened by falsifications because they represent failure by the theory; in contrast Popper saw a falsifying experiment as a success, opening up "new vistas in to a world of new experiences." (80). While Popper welcomed new arguments against the ruling theory the conventionalist is apt to see the bold new theory as a threat which might precipitate something like "the total collapse of science."

Popper noted four methods to protect a theoretical system from a prima facie refutation (1) ad hoc modifications to explain the result (2) modification of definitions in the system (3) questioning the validity of the experiment or the observation and (4) casting doubt on the acumen of the theoretician. He quoted Black (1803) "A nice adaptation of conditions will make almost any hypothesis agree with the phenomena. This will please our imagination but will not advance our knowledge" (82).

Methodological rules

Popper argued that analysis of the logical form of a system of statements would not reveal whether it is refutable or whether it is a "protected" conventional system and so it is a matter of methodological rules or decisions whether to use the protective devices or to expose the system to possible refutation. He wrote "The only way to avoid conventionalism is by taking a decision: the decision not to apply its method." (82). Since Kuhn advanced the theory of paradigms and normal science, it is apparent that protection of the ruling paradigm is the contemporary version of conventionalism, with an added protective device – the concept of incommensurability.

Popper's response to the first strategy, the use of ad hoc hypotheses, was to propose that these are only acceptable if they increase the testability of the system. An example was the postulation of the existence of another planet to explain some irregularities that were observed in the orbit of Uranus. This prediction was initially regarded as ad hoc but the precision of Newton's theory permitted astronomers to calculate where the missing planet should be found in the heavens.

Quite soon, two observers reported observations of a body which was named the planet Neptune. This turned an apparent challenge to the theory into a triumph.

Falsifiability and falsification

Popper drew a crucial distinction between *falsifiability* and *falsification*. Failure to understand this distinction has resulted in a lot of misrepresentation of Popper's ideas about falsifiability, especially since his philosophy of science became almost universally described as "falsificationism". Consequently concerns about the logic and the practice of falsification became central to the interpretation and teaching of Popper's philosophy, sometimes to the neglect of other aspects that are equally important, such as the rejection of subjectivism and the theory of conjectural knowledge.

> We must clearly distinguish between falsifiability and falsification. We have introduced falsifiability solely as a criterion for the empirical character of a system of statements. As to falsification, special rules must be introduced which will determine under what conditions a system is to be regarded as falsified. (86)

Falsifiability is thus a matter of logic, while falsification is a matter of practice. A strictly universal statement can be falsified by a single true observation statement which contradicts it—provided, of course, that the observation statement that contradicts it is actually true. Popper introduced a rule for falsification: *the effect has to be reproducible*. This is important in scientific practice because Polanyi and others have emphasised how often scientific laws are violated in the laboratory simply due to the vagaries of experimentation. That is why good practice calls for exhaustive description of the details of experimental procedures to permit important observations, such as the results of crucial experiments which may decide a contest between major hypotheses, to be repeated in other laboratories.

As noted above, no conclusive falsification of a theory can ever be produced due to the availability of the conventionalist strategies but this does not undermine the value of the critical method and the function of testing to locate areas where more work and new ideas are required.

Chapter V. The Problem of the Empirical Basis

Popper developed his ideas in debate with the logical positivists and this chapter demonstrates how he engaged with their central concern to locate the foundations of knowledge in sense impressions or sense data, especially sight. (Recall the old saying "seeing is believing").

To summarize the contents of the chapter; first a statement of Fries's trilemma followed by an incisive commentary on the protracted debate among the positivists on the matter of protocol sentences. He explained his turn from the subjective to the objective approach to the foundational problem. He exhaustively described the logical function of basic statements, building on the logical analysis of falsifiability and falsification in the previous chapter. He described what he called the relativity of basic statements and offered a resolution of Fries's trilemma. He addressed the logical relationship between theory and experiment, and the process of forming a critical preference for one theory rather than another which he compared with court proceedings where a jury is called to make a guilty or not guilty verdict.

Perceptual experiences as empirical basis: psychologism

The empirical or observational base has to be converted into statements for logical comparison with the statements that are deduced from the conjunction of the theory under test, ancillary theories, and statements of initial conditions. The positivists demanded an empirical basis in the form of sensory experience and this raised many issues about the treatment of these experiences to make them amenable to logical analysis.

Fries (1773-1843) was an early student of these matters. He suggested that to avoid dogmatic acceptance of the statements of science they need to be justified. If we try to justify them by argument we must resort to justifying statements by other statements which leads to an infinite regress. The third way out (to avoid *dogmatism* and the *infinite regress*) is *psychologism,* the claim that statements can be justified by perceptual experience. That is referred to as "Fries' trilemma".

Popper pointed out that the "perceptual basis" doctrine or "sensationalism, falls over on the problems of induction and of universals. The problem of induction arises if individual observations are supposed to generate universal generalizations by means of inductive logic.

Concerning the so-called protocol sentences

In the quest for the perceptual foundations of science the Vienna Circle conducted a serious and protracted debate about "protocol sentences" such as "I, Rafe at [time and place] observe [x]." Popper noted some of the variations that Carnap and Neurath rang on this theme without successfully demonstrating that the foundations of science could rest on indubitable sensations or unequivocal protocol statements.

Carnap addressed the forms of speech and especially the forms of the language of science to test the sentences of science with the help of protocol sentences which are supposed to describe the contents of immediate experience (the simplest known facts). Popper described that as psychologism translated into a formal mode of speech.

Neurath accepted that protocol sentences are not inviolable, which Popper regarded as a step in the right direction but he objected that Neurath did not explain how to decide whether a discordant protocol sentence should be deleted to protect the theoretical system, or the system should be altered to accommodate the protocol sentence.

The objectivity of the empirical base

Popper refused to be drawn into the debate on protocol sentences because he did not accept that there is a foundational basis for science in sensations—or anything else. He took a different turn (which can be described as his "objective turn"), starting with a sharp distinction between objective science and our subjective knowledge. That led to his view of the essential task of epistemology: "what epistemology has to ask is, rather: how do we test scientific statements by their deductive consequences?" (98).

He addressed the procedures required to permit inter-subjective, or public, testing of theories. That means describing the observational or experimental procedures in such a way that other people can repeat them. Assertions which cannot be tested due to their logical form may function as a stimulus for scientific investigation or for novel theoretical developments in logic and mathematics. This could apply to such things as reports of giant sea serpents or, in logic and mathematics, to Fermat's problem. Popper wrote that: "In such cases science does not say that the reports are unfounded or that Fermat was in error. Instead, it suspends judgment." (100).

Basic statements

In this section Popper explained the logical requirements for basic statements in his scheme and he prescribed the rule that basic statements have the form of singular existential statements. (102). They assert that an observable event is occurring at a specific point in space and time.

The relativity of basic statements and resolution of Fries's trilemma

The end point of testing is a basic statement which we (the experimenters) decide to accept. That is not a logical end point, there is always the possibility of more testing of the basic statements, using deductions from the statements in conjunction with some other theories. The procedure has no natural end.

Introducing the element of decision and Popper's reference to the relativity of basic statements might appear to be a concession to irrationalism or some form of arbitrary process. To signal that it is not a concession to relativism it might be described in the language of *relationships* rather than *relativity* because the stopping point is related to the state of the theoretical argument and stage of experimental testing. As noted, the testing can be extended and this provides a resolution of Fries's trilemma.

Popper conceded that the basic statements at the stopping point:

> have admittedly the character of dogmas, but only in so far as we may desist from justifying them by further arguments (or by further tests). But this kind of dogmatism is innocuous since, should the need arise, these statements can easily be tested further. (105)

One might ask whether it is appropriate to use the term dogma in that context. Popper's point is that the process of testing is in principle infinite but this process is not a regress because in Popper's scheme it is not supposed to provide foundations. The regress is innocuous, not vicious. At the same time it is not a concession to psychologism because there is no claim of justification by the basic statements.

> Experiences can motivate a decision, and hence an acceptance or rejection of a statement, but a basic statement cannot be justified by them – no more than by thumping the table. (105)

Theory and experiment

Against naïve empiricists and inductivists who believe in starting work by collecting facts (or observations) Popper insisted on the priority of theories which guide and motivate the experimental work and other forms of observation. He cited episodes where theorists predicted an observational effect which was only later produced (de Broglie's prediction of the wave character of matter) and progress which occurred in the wake of falsifications of accepted theories (the Michelson-Morley experiment). He observed that accidental discoveries occur but they are rare and usually they are picked up because the observers had "prepared minds" which were receptive to the phenomena which could otherwise have been ignored (penicillin).

Critical preference

Popper posed the question "How and why do we accept on theory in preference to others?"

> We choose the theory which best holds its own in competition with other theories: the one which, by natural selection, proves itself the fittest to survive. This will be the one which not only has hitherto stood up to the severest tests, but the one which is also testable in the most rigorous way. (108)

He noted the function of decisions in this process (with regard to the acceptance of basic statements) and he contrasted his position with that of conventionalists who adopt the criterion of simplicity for the acceptance of theories, (systems including universal statements). He agreed with the conventionalist that the choice of a theory is an act, a practical matter but he disagreed that aesthetic motives should be decisive, in the manner of the conventionalist.

He introduced the analogy of the courtroom procedure in trial by jury to explain the difference between a justification and a decision reached in a procedure governed by rules.

He ended the chapter with one of his trademark anti-foundational statements.

> The empirical basis of objective science has thus nothing 'absolute' about it. Science does not rest upon solid bedrock. The bold structure of its theories rises, as it were, above a swamp. It is like a building built on piles... and if we stop driving the piles deeper, it is not because we have reached firm ground. We simply stop when we are satisfied that the piles are firm enough to carry the structure, at least for the time being. (111)

An alternative explanation of the lack of foundations is to compare the empirical base with the mooring lines of a hot air balloon which is driven upwards by the 'hot air' of conjecture. The balloon is attached to the earth by thin deductive lines of argument which do not hold it up, they stop it from losing touch with the ground and drifting away.

In a 1972 addendum Popper noted that his term "basis" (the empirical base) has ironic overtones because it is a basis that is not firm!

Chapter VI. Degrees of Testability

In a 1972 addendum Popper drew attention to two points in this chapter. One is that the testability (and the content) of a theory may have degrees. The second is that the growth of knowledge can be identified with increasing content in our theories. He also noted that one of the very important ideas in the book is the empirical or information content of a theory. Section 7 of *Unended Quest*, the long digression on essentialism, expands on the ideas of the logical and information content of theories.

It is apparent that some hypotheses can be more easily tested than others, and that the difficulty is increased when the system under investigation is very large, very small, or very complex. This chapter is concerned with technical matters pertaining to testing, including; the class of potential falsifiers as analysed in terms of the cardinality (or power) of a class; the concept of the dimensions of the class; the structure of sub-class relations; empirical content, entailment and degrees of falsifiability; levels of universality, and degrees of precision. There is also a technical discussion of degrees of testability with reference to the dimensions of various sets of curves.

Chapter VII. Simplicity

At various times simplicity in theories has been highly prized but a number of technical issues are explored in this chapter to demonstrate that the aim of simplicity may raise more problems than it solves. Theories need to be sufficiently complex to account for the complexity of the system under investigation (bearing in mind that for analytical purposes specific aspects or parts of complex systems are usually isolated for investigation). For many practical and technological purposes theories which are known to be false can be used as instruments for applications and purposes where they have been well tested.

Chapter VIII. Probability and Chapter IX. Some Observations on Quantum Theory

As was noted at the outset, the amount of technical detail in these chapters is likely to trouble many general readers. Everyone needs to understand the Popperian "themes" and the way that these play out in their own areas of interest. But for most people it is probably sufficient to appreciate the broad outline of Popper's thinking on probability and physics.

These two chapters represent the first stage in Popper's long march to promote realism, objectivism and indeterminism in physics against the most influential interpretation of quantum theory which he considered to be under the influence of instrumentalism, determinism and the subjective interpretation of probability theory.

The march continued between 1934 and 1959 when the English translation appeared and over that time the major change in Popper's thinking was a shift from the frequency interpretation of probability to the propensity interpretation.

Some of the changes are signalled in new footnotes and the new appendices to *The Logic of Scientific Discovery*. The most up to date and comprehensive treatment of these matters is in the three volumes of the *Postscript to the Logic of Scientific Discovery* which was almost completed during the 1950s but only appeared in print in three volumes in the early 1980s.

The problems

The status of probabilities became critical in quantum theory and for Popper this posed the problem of testing (falsifying) probability statements.

> Thus we are confronted with two tasks. The first is to provide new foundations for the calculus of probability. The second task is to elucidate the relations between probability and experience. This means solving what I call the problem of decidability of probability statements. (146)

In the chapter on probability Popper argued against the subjective theory of probability which depicts probabilities as a reflection of our ignorance of the full details of the situation. Against this, Popper regarded distributions as observed facts and he showed how to make probability statements testable. Logically speaking they are not testable because whatever happens may be deemed a very rare part of some sequence or another, however improbable that part of our observed world might be, according to Bernoulli's law of great numbers etc.

Popper's proposal was to take as a convention (a rule of the game) the hypothesis that any observed sequence is not too improbable. This convention is standard, although the inductivists can make no sense of it. Popper's desideratum is that we invent testable hypotheses and test them, noting that the observations are samples (distributions) and not single events.

Popper also asked, which item belongs to a given ensemble? Usually, unless we specify the answer in observable terms we cannot apply the probability calculus. Thus there is no statistics of thefts; there are statistics of observed thefts, reported thefts, and estimated thefts, not of thefts as such. When we consider illness of children, for example, we may discuss whether children are prone to a given disease; this "proneness" is a disposition or propensity (and it may be altered by interventions).

Popper saw propensities as "soft" or "plastic", so for example nuclei have the propensity to disintegrate (to different degrees). And the numerical values of these degrees follow the calculus of probability. Against determinism, Popper talked about "plastic control" by the laws of nature in the essay "Of Clouds and Clocks" which is reprinted in *Objective Knowledge*.

Popper followed Keynes and Renyi and offered an autonomous axiom system for probability, that is probabilities of unspecified objects, in the way group theory discusses groups of unspecified objects. This was a significant mathematical achievement which has only lately been recognised when Hugh Leblanc showed that Popper's axioms have new unintended models.

In the chapter on quanta Popper tried to show that Heisenberg's principle, far from discouraging tests should be seen as a challenge to experimental scientists. Popper offered a sketch for such a test that was criticized by Heisenberg and by Einstein. The rectification of this experiment is due to Einstein, Podolsky and Rosen.

For further reading, Simkin's book *Popper's Views on Natural and Social Science* has a chapter "A World of Propensities" which sketches Popper's progress from his first attack on probability theory to the "world of propensities. Popper also wrote a book titled *A World of Propensities* (1990).

Thanks to Joe Agassi for assistance with these chapters.

Chapter X. Corroboration, or How a Theory Stands Up to Tests

Popper rejected the possibility of verifying theories, and also the fallback position of confirming them and the use of numerical probability measures. So he had to answer the question - what is achieved when a hypothesis passes empirical tests? His answer is the theory of corroboration.

He adopted this term (suggested by the New Zealand soil chemist Hugh Parton) to distance himself from Carnap who wanted to talk about the "degree of confirmation".

Most of this chapter is occupied with arguments against the idea of attaching numerical probability values to theories by means of inductive logic. One of the defences mounted by the inductivists is to appeal to the uniformity of nature as an "inductive principle" which we cannot live without. For Popper, the uniformity of nature has nothing to do with the logic of induction (attempting to put p values on theories) but,

> It expresses the metaphysical faith in the existence of regularities in our world (a faith which I share, and without which practical action

> is hardly conceivable). Yet the question before us - the question which makes the non-verifiability of theories significant in the present context - is on an altogether different plane.(252-3)

The plane that concerned Popper is the logic of testing and the way that the outcome of tests is inevitably uncertain due to the theory-dependence of observations, the Duhem problem and the like. And so the outcome for Popper is that corroboration is about reporting how well a hypothesis has "proved its mettle" by standing up to tests and solving whatever theoretical problem it was designed to address.

It may help at this point to consider what Bartley called "the check on the problem", that is to be clear about the problem that a theory of corroboration (or confirmation) is supposed to solve. Originally it was supposed to answer the question, "Is this theory true?" and later "Is this theory probable?" For Popper, operating with the theory of conjectural knowledge and also considering what he called "the essential incompleteness of all science" (in an Addendum to the second volume of the *Postscript to The Logic of Scientific Discovery*), the purpose of testing depends on the situation: there may need to be a choice for a practical or technological application, or there may need to be a decision about the next steps in a research program.

Appendix. Some laws for the republic of science

The "supreme rule" and the first two subsidiary rules were proposed by Popper. Jarvie (2000) identified additional rules which can be found scattered in the text of Popper's book.

First the supreme or meta-rule that governs the other rules.

SR. The other rules of scientific procedure must be designed in such a way that they do not protect any statement in science from falsification (*LScD*, 54).

R1. The game of science is, in principle, without end. He who decides one day that scientific statements do no call for further test, and that they can be regarded as finally verified, retires from the game (*LScD*, 53).

R2. Once a hypothesis has been proposed and tested, and has proved its mettle, it may not be allowed to drop out without 'good reason' (*LScD*, 53-54).

R3. We are not to abandon the search for universal laws and for a coherent theoretical system, nor ever give up our attempts to explain causally any kind of event we can describe (*LScD*, 61).

R4. I shall...adopt a rule not to use undefined concepts as if they were implicitly defined (*LScD*, 75).

R5. Only those auxiliary hypotheses are acceptable whose introduction does not diminish the degree of falsifiability or testability of the system in question but, on the contrary, increases it (*LScD*, 83).

R6. We shall forbid surreptitious alterations of usage (*LScD*, 84).

R7. Inter-subjectively testable experiments are either to be accepted, or to be rejected in the light of counter-experiments (*LScD*, 84).

R8. The bare appeal to logical derivations to be discovered in future can be disregarded (*LScD*, 84).

R9. After having produced some criticism of a rival theory, we should always make a serious attempt to apply this criticism to our own theory (*LScD*, 85n).

R10. We should not accept stray basic statements - i.e logically disconnected ones – but...we should accept basic statements in the course of testing theories; or raising searching questions about these theories, to be answered by the acceptance of basic statements (*LScD*, 106).

R11. This makes our methodological rule that those theories should be given preference which can be most severely tested...equivalent to a rule favouring theories with the highest possible empirical content (*LScD*, 121).

R12. I propose that we take the methodological decision never to explain physical effects, i.e. reproducible regularities, as accumulations of accidents (*LScD*, 199).

R13. A rule...which might demand that the agreement between basic statements and the probability estimate should conform to some minimum standard. Thus the rule might draw some arbitrary line and decree that only reasonably representative segments (or reasonably 'fair samples') are 'permitted', while a-typical or non-representative segments are 'forbidden' (*LScD*, 204).

R14. The rule that we should see whether we can simplify or generalize or unify our theories by employing explanatory hypotheses of the type mentioned (that is to say, hypotheses explaining observable effects as summations or integrations of micro events) (*LScD*, 207).

CHAPTER FOUR

THE OPEN SOCIETY AND ITS ENEMIES

CONTENTS

Why *The Open Society and Its Enemies* matters

The *Open Society and Its Enemies* is a systematic investigation of some powerful ideas which undermine our freedoms and the traditions of rationality and tolerance, especially during social and political crises. Popper set out to combine the best elements of social democracy (left liberalism) and classical (minimum state) liberalism to resolve a number of issues which confuse and divide the friends of freedom.

Wartime is the most dangerous time for erosion of freedoms and the rhetoric of war is often recruited to support tactics and policies that would not normally be considered during peacetime. Lately we have had the war on drugs and the war on terror. In the last 150 years the most damaging and divisive example of the rhetoric of war is the Marxist doctrine of the class war and Isiah Berlin described *The Open*

Society and Its Enemies as the most searching critique of Marxism in the English language.

Popper wrote the book under difficult circumstances while the outcome of WW2 was in doubt and sixteen of his relatives were engulfed in the Holocaust. His New Zealand friend and colleague Colin Simkin considered that the work was not only an intellectual achievement but also "a triumph of the human spirit," (Simkin, 1993, Appendix I). It can be seen as a counterpart to the Battle of Britain where young men took to the air in the skies over the south of England with the future of civilization virtually in their hands. On the other side of the world the relatively young Popper patrolled the stratosphere of the world of ideas to provide air support for the footsoldiers of the open society.

The problem of reception

The book was well received when it first appeared at the end of the war and it exerted considerable influence but nowadays it is practically invisible in academia and it has been kept in print by a lay readership. The critique of selected elements of Plato and Aristotle scandalized conservatives, despite Popper's high regard for their achievements. Similarly,his demolition of Marx upset radicals, despite the compliments that Popper paid to Marx.

The origin of *The Open Society and Its Enemies*

After Popper's *Logik der Forschung* launched in 1935 his focus shifted from the philosophy of science (focussed on physics) to politics and the social sciences. His major concern as a man of the moderate left was the failure of Marxism to provide a bastion against the rise of fascism. He attributed this more than anything to an intellectual error, especially the doctrine of historical inevitability which he called "historicism". He returned to his notes on "the poverty of historicism" after he moved to Canterbury College, Christchurch, New Zealand in 1937 and it became his war work after Hitler invaded Austria in 1938.

Section 10 of *The Poverty of Historicism* is devoted to a critique of "essentialism", the obsession with the correct definition of terms. In the course of researching and writing that section Popper found that his notes were growing until he stopped work on *The Poverty of Historicism* and instead wrote a more expansive book, which grew into *The Open Society and Its Enemies*.

The travails of Ernst Gombrich

Popper completed the book in January 1943 and then found that the very large and controversial manuscript was hard to place with a publisher. Eventually he obtained assistance from the Austrian art historian Ernst Gombrich and also from Friedrich Hayek, who were both in England. Finally Herbert Read, poet, historian, philosopher and editor at Routledge, accepted the book.

Ernst Gombrich had the major burden of seeing the book through the press. He told his story in the book *The Open Society After Fifty Years* (Jarvie and Pralong, 1999). Popper "assisted" in the process by sending some 95 aerograms with instructions on the finishing touches for the massive manuscript. On one occasion he posted twelve aerograms on a single day. On another occasion he completely rewrote chapter 17. When Routledge decided to produce the book in two volumes Gombrich cabled Karl "Routledge want division after Chapter 10". The local censor called Gombrich to the post office for an interview about the message and fortunately he accepted the explanation that they were not talking about troop movements!

When Popper was applying for various university positions in New Zealand and Australia he wrote to Gombrich:

> You kindly advise me to prefer Otago to Perth, in spite of the Cangeroos [sic]. But I think you don't really know enough of Australia by far: the nicest animal there (and possibly the loveliest animal that exists) is the Koala bear. Cangeroos may be nice, but the opportunity of seeing a Koala bear is worth putting up with anything, and it is without reservation my strongest motive in

wishing to go to Australia." (Gombrich, 2003, 24)

Finally, in a letter dated 16 November 1945.

> Dear Ernst, This time we are really off, I think…The passage will be very rough since we sail via Cape Horn – perhaps the roughest spot in all the Seven Seas. Our corpses are expected to arrive, by the New Zealand Star, on January 8th or thereabouts. Please receive them kindly. (*ibid*, 26)

In the event, Popper and his wife walked off the boat to meet the Gombrichs, and Ernst had a "hot off the press" copy of *The Open Society* in his hand.

The architecture of *The Open Society*

Popper covered a huge amount of ground in areas outside his previous concerns in science, mathematics and the philosophy of science. The first volume is concerned with the spell of Plato and the second, mostly on Marx, is subtitled "the high tide of prophecy", a residue of his original concern with the myth of historical determinism.

Western thought has been described as a series of footnotes to Plato. This is a tribute to his achievement and to the way that his ideas continue to exert influence to the present day. Many of our problems in politics and the social sciences are complicated by methods and doctrines that we have inherited from him.

Some of these are:

Excessive concern with the "correct" definition of terms (which Popper called essentialism).

The idea that individualism and altruism are not compatible.

The idea that "who shall rule?" is the most important question in political philosophy.

The quest for a utopian society by means of violent and revolutionary reform.

In the first volume he first described the beginning of the myth of origin and destiny, then Plato's descriptive sociology (where he found a class analysis), then Plato's political program including his theories of justice, leadership and social reform. Finally he examined the turbulent history of the time to explain why Plato was so desperately concerned to draft a blueprint for a stable state. The second volume starts with chapters on Aristotle and Hegel, then moves on to Marx's methods, and ends with chapters on the sociology of knowledge, rationality and the meaning of history (if any).

In some ways the reception of volume 1 has been distorted by the historicist label that Popper attached to Plato and there is a mass of literature that disputes Popper's interpretation of Plato (and Hegel and Marx as well). This distracts attention from the value of Popper's ideas in our daily task of devising and strengthening the traditions and institutions that make for peace, freedom and prosperity. The gloss that I have put on Popper's work in this field (like that of Hayek) is that he was concerned with the critical review and reform of the rules of the game of social and political life. It is not hard to envisage better rules of the game which lead in the direction of peace, freedom and prosperity, but massive amounts of energy have been devoted to installing and defending rules that lead in the opposite direction. This is where Popper's ideas have direct application at present.

From the Preface to the first edition (1945)

> If in this book harsh words are spoken about some of the greatest among the intellectual leaders of mankind, my motive is not, I hope, the wish to belittle them. It springs rather from my conviction that, if our civilization is to survive, we must break with the habit of deference to great men. Great men may make great mistakes...

From the Preface to the revised edition (1950)

Seen in the darkness of the present world situation, the criticism of Marxism which it attempts is liable to stand out as the main point of the book. This view of it is not wholly wrong and perhaps unavoidable, although the aims of the book are much wider. Marxism is only an episode—one of the many mistakes we have made in the perennial and dangerous struggle for building a better and freer world.

I see now more clearly than ever before that even our greatest troubles spring from something that is as admirable and sound as it is dangerous—from our impatience to better the lot of our fellows.

Introduction

Popper noted that the book raises issues which may not be apparent from the table of contents. One of the signature ideas of the book is the "strain of civilization", that is the unease and distress which many people experience during times of rapid social change. The problem of tribalism and the interface between tribal societies and their neighbours has assumed fresh significance with the rise of radical Islam. It may be that some of Popper's thoughts on the strain of the transition from a closed to an open society may have fresh relevance. The same applies to his discussion of the abuses of power, such as restrictions on free speech, which governments are tempted to use to maintain control in troubled times.

Chapter 1: Historicism and the Myth of Destiny

Historians can be divided into those who think that history consists of one damn thing after another, and the others who depict history as the revelation of a Great Plan. In this chapter Popper sketched the loosely connected body of ideas that he labelled historicism. The central idea is historical determinism, and various ideas that are closely related to it such as the doctrine of the "chosen people" who are the prime movers driving events, far over the heads of the common people who are merely pawns in the great game of History. What really counts are the great nations, the great leaders, or the great classes. Popper noted some of the ancient "chosen people" myths and the characteristics that they share with the two major modern (and secular) versions of the idea – racialism or fascism on one side and Marxist historical philosophy on the other.

That was written in the 1940s. One would have hoped that the collapse of fascism, the implosion of communism and the decline of belief in historical determinism (in no small measure due to Popper's influence) would have relegated *The Open Society* to the history of ideas. But old errors and old ways of thinking persist and many of the ideas which Popper subjected to criticism are still alive, albeit not in the virulent forms of totalitarianism. Democracy is still seen as majority rule, not limited government, Governments readily resort to "orders" to achieve short-term goals instead of "rules" which provide continuity and stability in government. Essentialism still rules in large tracts of the human sciences. And the rise of radical Islam and the stirring of Russian nationalism pose once more the problems of "the chosen people" and the myth of destiny.

Chapter 2: Heraclitus

This short chapter notes some of the Greek antecedents of Plato. Hesiod was a pessimist who thought that mankind was doomed to degenerate, both physically and morally, from the mythical Golden Age. Heraclitus is a more ambivalent figure who anticipated many of the complex and confused doctrines of some modern thinkers such as Hegel.

Chapter 3: Plato's Theory of Forms or Ideas

The theory of Forms or Ideas has at least three different and overlapping functions in Plato's scheme. First, it is central to his theory of knowledge which depends on gaining access to the "essence of things" in the World of Ideas or Unchanging Forms. Second, it provides the regularities that maintain continuity behind the chaos and confusion of an ever-changing world. Thirdly it provides a rationalization for the quest to achieve the unchanging social order which approximates to the Ideal of the State.

A note on the notes

Popper wanted to solve some fundamental problems rather than to popularize them and to help the general reader he put a great deal of technical material to the notes in the back the book. In the Plato volume there are 200 pages of text and 120 pages of footnotes in smaller print. In the second volume he only managed 90 pages of notes to accompany 280 pages of text. Some of the notes are full-blooded essays that run for several pages and could have been published as journal articles. These include a critical account of the early work of Wittgenstein, a suggestion as to how Germany could have been treated after World War I to minimise inconvenience for the people while rendering the nation incapable of launching another war, his first moves towards the theory of metaphysical research programs and a critical essay on "scientific" moral theories.

Essentialism

This chapter contains a preliminary exposition and some criticism of the concern with definitions and the essential meaning of concepts which Popper called essentialism. This topic triggered the shelving of *The Poverty of Historicism* and the writing of *The Open Society and Its Enemies*.

> I use the name methodological essentialism to characterize the view, held by Plato and many of his followers, that it is the task of pure knowledge or 'science' to discover and to describe the true nature of things, i.e. their hidden reality or essence. It was Plato's peculiar belief that the essence of sensible things can be found in other and more real things—in their primogenitors or Forms. (31)

For the essentialist there are three ways of knowing something: (1) to know or recognise the essence, (2) to know the definition and (3) to know the name.

Chapter 11 contains a more detailed account of the Aristotelian method of definition by essences. Popper argued that excessive concern with terms and definitions is a significant error of method in the humanities and social sciences.

Chapter 4: Change and Rest

This chapter contains Popper's interpretation of Plato's political program as a plan to arrest change and create a stable, totalitarian state. A significant body of thought had to be defeated in Athens to win hearts and minds to this task. These are the ideas of the Great Generation of Athens, a movement whose spirit is captured in the funeral oration of Pericles. An extract from the speech can be found at the end of this chapter.

The Achilles heel of Athens may have been its empire and the heavy-handed way it treated its foreign dominions and its allies. That gives the story of the Great Generation an extra dimension of contemporary relevance.

In Popper's account Plato developed a systematic history and sociology of the Greek states to interpret the turbulent political world around him. Plato drew on the ancient civilizations of Sparta and Crete to re-create a model of the ancient or original state before it was corrupted and disrupted by internal conflict and social change. The Republic represents his model state.

Popper suggested that Plato's achievement as a pioneer in sociology has been largely overlooked because his theories about the origins of society and the evolution of political systems organisation are connected with his ethical and political demands. Examples of his speculative historical reconstructions include:

- A theory of the primitive beginnings of society, of tribal patriarchy, and the typical periods in the development of social life.

- Insights into the role of the economic background of political life and historical development; according to Popper a theory revived by Marx under the name historical materialism.

- The law of political revolutions, according to which all revolutions presuppose a disunited ruling class or elite.

The chapter contains five sections, of which the fifth is a short summary.

Section I shows how Plato used the Theory of Forms to provide the foundation for his history, his sociological analysis and his political program.

In Section II Popper described Plato's theory of revolution and stability, with some comments on the way the story changed somewhat over several dialogues as Plato's Socrates drifted from the historical democrat towards the rather different figure who was the primary mouthpiece for Plato's anti-democratic views. For the mature Plato, the history of the state is a picture of degeneration from perfection, precipitated by disunity of the rulers, through a series of stages. First, on the way down, timocracy (the rule of the noble), then oligarchy (the rule of the rich), then democracy (the rule of the many) and finally, tyranny

For Plato, democracy is only one step removed from the worst of all worlds and he turned all his rhetorical skills against it. The key to stability and maintenance of the model state is to maintain the solidarity of the ruling class and their capacity of withstand both foreign enemies and the revolt of the lower classes.

Section III gives an unsympathetic sketch for the Ideal State, the Republic, often interpreted as a progressive Utopia. The main thing is to avoid class war and so the structure is a rigid hierarchy, with the rulers and their auxiliaries at the top and the remainder of the population virtually enslaved below. The mass of the people were of no interest to Plato and he even went to the extreme of prohibiting the rulers to legislate for the lower orders or have any concern for their petty problems.

To ensure the internal unity of the rulers, the master class, there is special education (treated in the next section and the chapter on Leadership) and there is communism to eliminate economic interests. The State itself would be self-contained and isolated, with no trade and commerce with other nations. All property is to be held in common and the same applies to women and children. Here is a truly remarkably progressive program to eliminate the family!

> No member of the ruling class must be able to identify his children, or his parents. The family must be destroyed, or rather, extended to cover the whole warrior class. Family loyalties might otherwise become a possible source of disunion; therefore 'each should look upon all as if belonging to one family'. (48)

Section IV describes the origin, breeding and education of the ruling class. The origin is very much a matter of mythology and Plato speculated about the conquest of farmers by a warrior class of hunters. Here we encounter the strong element of racialism in Plato's thought. The rulers were essentially a master race and it was vital to maintain the purity of the race along with internal unity and an overwhelming monopoly on power. "To this end, it is important that the master class should feel as one superior master race. 'The race of the guardians must be kept pure', says Plato (in defence of infanticide)."(51).

One of the problems that Plato had to address was the need to instil the right balance of fierceness and gentleness in the rulers so they could handle dangers from inside and outside the State, without being aggressive with each other or monstering the human sheep. The right breeding is essential and also a judicious balance between music and gymnastics in the education of the young. There are some amusing restrictions on the kind of music that is acceptable and there are less amusing limits placed on poets who would be subjected to strict censorship with the threat of banishment from the State if they undermined the obedience and loyalty of the people.

Extracts from the Funeral Oration of Pericles .
https://online.hillsdale.edu/document.doc?id=355

We do not copy our neighbours but try to be an example. Our administration favours the many instead of the few: this is why it is called a democracy. The law affords equal justice to all alike in their private disputes, but we do not ignore the claims of excellence

The freedom we enjoy extends also to ordinary life; we are not suspicious of one another, and do not nag our neighbour if he chooses to go his own way. But this freedom does not make us lawless. We are taught to respect the magistrates and the laws, and never to forget that we must protect the injured. And we are also taught to observe those unwritten laws whose sanction lies only in the universal feeling of what is right.

Our city is thrown open to the world; we never expel a foreigner. We are free to live exactly as we please, and yet we are always ready to face any danger.

We love beauty without indulging in fancies, and although we try to improve our intellect, this does not weaken our will.

To admit one's poverty is no disgrace with us; but we consider it disgraceful not to make an effort to avoid it.

We consider a man who takes no interest in the state not as harmless, but as useless; and although only a few may originate a policy, we are all able to judge it.

We believe that happiness is the fruit of freedom and freedom that of valour, and we do not shrink from the dangers of war.

To sum up, I think that Athens is the School of Hellas, and that the individual Athenian grows up to develop a happy versatility, a readiness for emergencies, and self-reliance.

Chapter 5: Nature and Convention

> Man has created new worlds - of language, of music, of poetry, of science; and the most important of these is the world of the moral demands, for equality, for freedom, and for helping the weak. (65)

Popper is not usually regarded as contributor to moral philosophy, although someone compiled a lexicon of technical philosophical terms with an entry "Popper, (verb):- As in To philosophise in a tone of high moral seriousness, the converse of which is Impopper."

This chapter serves three purposes.

First, Popper set out his views on critical dualism in morals, that is the distinction between unchangeable *laws* of nature and manmade *rules and regulations*. More importantly, he explained that this does mean that our laws and conventions are arbitrary or irrational so that that any system is as good as any other (cultural relativism).

Second, he described how the emergence of critical dualism is one of the important differences between a closed or tribal society and a more open and pluralistic society. At the personal level this attitude is something that we would expect to see developing in young people as they grow up.

Third, he showed how Plato blurred the distinction between natural laws and human conventions to support his political program.

Critical dualism

Critical dualism is the view that there is no way to derive moral principles from matters of fact. In the language of moral philosophy this is often called "the is/ought problem. The problem arises when philosophers want to find some way to justify moral principles on the basis of some set of facts. As Popper pointed out in note 18 to this chapter, almost everyone who has dealt with this issue has tried to answer it by reference to human nature or to the nature of "the good". But each of these forks leads to a dead end: the first because anything that anyone does can be attributed to human nature and the second because there is always the question of defining the good.

To clarify his own position Popper briefly stated what he regarded as the most important principles of humanitarian and equalitarian ethics.

First, "tolerance towards all who are not intolerant and who do not propagate intolerance. So the moral decisions of others should be treated with respect, as long as such decisions do not conflict with the principle of tolerance."(Chapter 5, note 6). He noted that there is a paradox of tolerance, meaning that if tolerance on the part of the tolerant has no limits then the intolerant may rise up and destroy the tolerant and tolerance at the same time. In a paper published long after *The Open Society and its Enemies* (but written at the same time) he wrote:

> I have insisted that we must be tolerant. But I also believe that this tolerance has its limits. We must not trust those anti-humanitarian religions which not only preach destruction but act accordingly. For if we tolerate them, then we become ourselves responsible for their deeds. (Popper, 2008, 47-48)

The issue of the limits of tolerance has become topical with the emergence of radical Islam and the problem of working out a coherent response to its friends, supporters and apologists in the west.

Second. "The recognition that all moral urgency has its basis in the urgency of suffering or pain". Popper replaced the utilitarian formula 'Aim at the greatest amount of happiness for the greatest number', or briefly, 'Maximize happiness' with what some have called reverse utilitarianism which is summed up by the formula 'The least amount of avoidable suffering for all', or briefly, 'Minimize suffering'." (Chapter 5, note 6).

Third, "to resist tyranny by safeguarding the other principles by the institutional means of a legislation rather than by the benevolence of persons in power." (Chapter 5, note 6).

For those who have no argument with critical dualism there is little more to be gained from most of this chapter which has largely academic interest either for those with a special interest in the logic of the is/ought problem or the works of Plato.

The chapter has nine sections.

Sections I and III set out Popper's statement of the dualism between is and ought, or between propositions and proposals, backed up by some very heavy arguments in the notes. In section II he speculated about shift from the time when people made no distinction between laws of nature and human rules and conventions.

Section IV introduces Popper's idea about sociological laws connected with the functioning of social institutions. These have the character of natural laws and he considered them to be the appropriate subject matter for sociology as a social science. (See Chapter 9 on social reform.) Section V is an account of some intermediate steps in the development from naive or magical monism to critical dualism.

Section VI examines the relationship between Plato's use of various forms of naturalism to support his political program. Section VII briefly sketches Plato's analogy of the city with a human body, so that politics can be regarded as a form of social hygiene.

Section VIII outlines one of Plato's more far-fetched stories to explain the process of social and political degeneration. It is called the theory of Numbers and the Fall of Man, and it connects to his ideas about selective breeding to maintain the racial purity of the guardians.

Section VIII spells out the metaphysical ground-plan of Plato's enterprise.

Chapter 6: Totalitarian Justice

Plato promoted a highly influential and damaging theory of totalitarian or collectivist justice as an alternative to equalitarian or individualist theory.

He propagated the idea that individualism is not compatible with altruism.

He exploited defective arguments which are often used to defend the protective state and equalitarian justice. These weaknesses are the theory of natural rights and the social contract theory of human society. The equalitarian theory needs to be described in the language of political proposals, in the context of the protective state.

Organisation of the chapter

The introduction to the chapter outlines Plato's program and notes how it has been idealized, even by some writers who were aware of its dangerous tendencies.

Section I describes how Plato recast the theory of justice to mean protecting the stability and the class structure of the state.

Section II raises and dismisses the suggestion that Plato's theory of totalitarian justice corresponded with the customary Greek meaning of the term.

Section III restates the three key elements of the equalitarian theory which Popper supported and their opposites, which Plato defended.

Section IV states the program (articulated by Pericles in his funeral speech) of rejecting all doctrines of natural privilege and shows how Plato attacked this.

Section V defends the principle of individualism versus collectivism and shows how Plato's brilliant rhetoric managed to identify individualism with selfishness, and altruism with collectivism. This leads to totalitarianism when combined with other elements of Plato's program, including his theory of leadership.

Section VI explains the theory of the protective state, in contrast with Plato's theory that the state is all-important. It also explains the language of political proposals as an alternative to the defective and confusing methods of essentialism and historicism. Essentialism means trying to establish the true meaning of terms (such as freedom and justice) and historicism is the error of explanation by origins, sometimes called the genetic fallacy.

Section VII shows how the equalitarian theory of justice and the protective state were expounded by a younger contemporary of Plato. The ideas only survive in fragments of Plato's early work and in some critical commentaries by Aristotle.

Section VIII explains the rhetorical devices that Plato used in his later and most influential works on politics (*Republic* and *Laws*) to suppress or misrepresent the ideas of individual freedom and equalitarian justice in favour of his own collectivist program.

From the top of the chapter

Popper argued that Plato's political programme follows from his overwhelming concern with stability. To achieve that, Plato proposed that the utopian republic should have rigid class rule including:

- The strict division of the classes.

- The identification of the fate of the state with that of the ruling class.

- The ruling class has a monopoly of military training and of the right to carry arms.

- Censorship is strict to prevent the propagation of subversive ideas, even in the fictional vehicles of poetry and drama.

- There is continual propaganda, starting with the education of young children.

- There is no trade with other states to avoid dependence on traders and other states.

In Popper's opinion, the program can be fairly described as totalitarian. He noted some objections to that verdict, such as Plato's desire for Goodness and Beauty, and his love of Wisdom and Truth, and the idea that the wise should rule, rather than the strong or a hereditary monarch. And above all is the idea that the state should be founded upon Justice. These objections reflect the tendency to interpret Plato in the best possible light, even on the part of writers who were clearly aware of the totalitarian tendencies in his thinking.

Popper defended equalitarian justice by which he meant equality before non-discriminatory laws and an equal distribution of the limitations on freedom that are required for a functional society.

Plato's *Republic* is probably the most influential book on justice until *On Justice* by Rawls in 1972. It underpins the programs of both outright totalitarians and also the program of socialist "social justice" which also undermines equalitarian justice in a slower but equally deadly manner.

For Popper, Platonic justice means keeping your place in the social hierarchy. In contrast, Popper summed up equalitarian and individualistic justice with three main proposals:

- The elimination of "natural" privileges in favour of particular people or groups over others.

- The principle of individualism. Justice applies to individuals rather than groups.

- A major function of the state is to protect the freedom of individuals, not to promote conformity.

Plato, in opposition, supported the principle of natural privilege, holism or collectivism, and the imperative of maintaining the stability of the realm.

Equalitarianism is the demand that the citizens of the state should be treated impartially, that is, they should be equal under the law. It is important to note that this is a proposal and if it is not realised in fact, it still remains an objective and it is not a criticism of the proposal to point out that there may be "one law for the rich and another for the poor."

Plato's principle of justice was, of course, diametrically opposed to all this. He demanded natural privileges for the natural leaders. But how did he contest the equalitarian principle? And how did he establish his own demands?

Plato exploited some of the best-known formulations of the equalitarian demands, especially those which were spelled out in the language of natural rights, and the natural (biological) equality of men. This is unhelpful because people are equal in some respects and very unequal in others. Further, as explained in the previous chapter, nothing follows from the facts of the matter in any case.

Individualism and collectivism

Popper began his exposition with some examination of the terminology. He found that the Oxford Dictionary defined individualism in two different ways. One is the opposite of collectivism, and the other is the opposite of altruism. He used "individualism" in the first sense and for the second he preferred to use quite different terms such as "egoism" or "selfishness". He drew up a table to make the point.

(a) Individualism is opposed to (a') Collectivism.

(b) Egoism is opposed to (b') Altruism

Plato collapsed the categories in the table to make a case for the inevitable conflict or tension between individualism and altruism. The table shows that is not necessarily so. Collectivism is not opposed to egoism, nor is it identical with altruism or unselfishness. And an anti-collectivist, (an individualist), can be willing to make sacrifices to help others.

For people who follow Plato's view on the matter, there is no such thing as altruistic individualism or a person who is well disposed to others (altruistic) and opposes collectivism. The four possibilities in the table are collapsed into two and that perception has created difficulties in coming to grips with ethical matters to the present day. For example the psychoanalytical revisionist Ian D. Suttie explained how Freud's theoretical system struggled to provide a simple explanation for friendly and sociable behaviour (Suttie, year, chapter). Decades later, much the same objections arose in response to Maslow's account of "self-actualizing people" who harmoniously blended individualistic and sociable characteristics.

The identification of individualism with egoism enabled Plato to criticize individualism and defend collectivism by appealing to the sentiment of unselfishness.

The language of political proposals and the protective theory of the state

Popper's positive contribution at this point was to clarify two things. One is the theory of the humanitarian, protective state. The other is an application of his "rules of the game" approach, to use the language of political demands or proposals to discuss policy, instead of the language of essentialism or historicism.

> In a clear presentation of this theory, *the language of political demands or of political proposals should be used*; that is to say, we should not try to answer the essentialist question: What is the state, what is its true nature, its real meaning? Nor should we try to answer the historicist question: How did the state originate, and what is the origin of political obligation? We should rather put our question in this way: What do we demand from a state? What do we propose to consider as the legitimate aim of state activity? (109)

This means making an all-important distinction between aggression and defence, even if some cases are difficult to decide and this may call for serious historical research. It means that constraints on freedom which can be justified to protect individuals and communities from criminals must apply to everyone, and the constraints must be the minimum that are necessary, such as limits on free speech in times of war.

It means that we need to have "rules of engagement" for the use of violence by the state both in defence of the realm and in policing law and order in the state. It also means formulating rules for revolutionary violence in the extreme situation where the rulers cannot be dismissed by democratic means.

Chapter 7: Leadership

The chapter has five sections. In the first Popper advanced two lines of argument against the idea that the question "who shall rule?" is the fundamental problem of political philosophy.

In section II he briefly outlined his alternative approach to the theory of democracy.

In section III he presented additional arguments for an institutional approach to democracy, in preference to theories that place too much emphasis on the short-term issue of leadership and majority rule.

In section IV he examined Plato's theory of the leadership of the wise and in section V he launched an attack on the system of education that Plato proposed to prepare the philosopher kings for their role.

The question "who shall rule the state?" has generally been accepted as a fundamental, if not *the* fundamental question in the philosophy and practice of politics. Popper dissented from that tradition and suggested that it has resulted in permanent confusion about the realistic and rational objectives of democratic political reform.

The first problem with that question is that the quest for the correct answer will distract attention from more helpful activities. At the very least we can consider an alternative approach, to be prepared for the bad leaders even while we try to find good ones. That means replacing the question Who shall rule? by a very different one, along the lines - how can we organize political institutions which minimize the damage that bad or incompetent leaders can inflict?

The "who shall rule" question follows from the assumption that political power is essentially unchecked, so that the rulers or the ruling party can do as they like. From this assumption it follows that the only important question is indeed "who is to be the sovereign?" Popper pointed out that even the most powerful dictators depend on their secret police, their henchmen and their hangmen. He then demonstrated that all theories of sovereignty are logically paradoxical because they do not handle the situation where, for argument sake, we think that the state should be ruled by the Good, and the Good decide that the state should be ruled by the Wise? Or if a democratic state votes a dictator into power?

A non-paradoxical proposal for democratic leadership

In section II Popper sketched a non-paradoxical theory which is not based on any assumption about the intrinsic goodness of majority rule, but rather on a decision to avoid and resist tyranny. He drew a distinction between two types of government: the first type can be dismissed or replaced without bloodshed, by peaceful constitutional means such as general elections. The second type consists of governments which cannot be changed by any means short of a successful revolution. Ludwig Mises used a similar definition of democracy in *Liberalism* (1927).

Using those two labels, the leading principle of democratic policy is nothing like "majority rule", it calls for the invention, development and protection of political institutions (and, equally important, traditions) *to control the abuse of power of all kinds*. We do not have to think that we can ever have a system of institutions and traditions which will never fail. We do not have to claim that the policies generated in the democratic process will be good. Popper simply argued that it is better to accept, for the time being, a bad policy in a democracy, than a good one in a dictatorship. The dictator may appear to be wise and benevolent but there is always the problem of the dictator's successor and the problem of remaining wise and benevolent while holding practically unlimited power and influence.

Personal and institutional issues

Many people expect too much of democracy, especially from being able to vote, as though elections are the be all and end all of good government. The more successful democracies tend to have a cluster of institutions and traditions as well as the franchise and regular elections. Among those traditions and institutions are freedom of speech and association, relatively efficient and non-corrupt police and courts, and a tradition of public service and fair play in the community at large. In a speech to the Mont Pelerin Society in 1954 Popper emphasized the vital function of the moral framework of society (Popper, 1963, Chapter 17). Notturno noted that Popper distinguished the open society from democracy, given the danger of the tyranny of the majority, and he emphasised "human freedom, fallibilism and the respect that we should have for the ideas of others." (Notturno, 2000, 88).

Popper noted that the institutions cannot improve themselves, that is the task of the citizens and those who criticize democracy on moral grounds fail to distinguish between personal and institutional problems. In the short term we may wish for better leaders, in the long term we need better institutions. This raises a fairly substantial budget of issues for the improvement of democracy, and too much is expected of the voting process itself, without regard to the way that the function of elections has been corrupted by what W. H. Hutt identified as "the vote-buying motive" when politicians find that they can buy votes using the taxpayers' money.

The remainder of chapter 7 is devoted to a number of critical comments on some aspects of Platonic education. These include Plato's plan to use the education system to prepare future leaders; progressive and romantic notions about educating for self development rather than learning; and the risk that a State monopoly on education will result in brainwashing and loss of diversity.

Chapter 8: The Philosopher King

Chapter 8 is a pendant to the chapter on leadership with more details on the breeding, training and method of operation of the philosopher kings. Plato used the role of the physician to explain why it is so important to maintain the organic unity of the state and to subordinate the individual to the collective. *The concept of the "noble" or "lordly" lie is introduced as an important propaganda device* to mislead the people and to impress them with useful fabrications such as the Myth of the Blood and Soil. According to this story the warriors who founded the city were supposed to be born of the earth instead of human mothers so they were completely dedicated to the defence of the city.

Chapter 9: Perfectionism, Utopianism

> Everything has got to be smashed to start with. Our whole damned civilization has got to go, before we can bring any decency into the world —'Mourlan', in Du Gard's *Les Thibaults*.

> All citizens above the age of ten must be expelled from the city and deported somewhere into the country; and the children who are now free from the influence of the manners and habits of their parents must be taken over. – Plato.

This chapter runs to only 12 pages and it contains some of the most important arguments in the whole book because countless millions of lives have been ruined by the application of the principles of revolutionary utopian reform. It is helpful to read this chapter with the image of Pol Pot's Cambodia and Mao's China in mind. Popper found a very dangerous approach to social reform in Plato; he called it Utopian engineering and he drew a contrast with another approach which he labelled piecemeal engineering.

The piecemeal reformer will seek to address the most urgent evils of society instead of aiming to achieve the greatest ultimate good, and this may look like a verbal quibble but Popper argued that it is the difference between a reasonable method of improving the lot of man, and a method which may easily lead to an intolerable increase in human suffering.

The case for utopian engineering runs like this: to act rationally we need to have an aim (an end), and then actions can be classified as rational if they are consistent with that end. By this logic, political actions are rational if they pursue the final end that has been set for the reform of the state. In that way, actions are driven by our ultimate political ends.

There is no scope for tolerance between different Utopian religions so the Utopian must either convert or destroy his Utopian rivals. Indeed it may not be enough to merely destroy the opposition, it may be deemed necessary to stamp out the very memory of it. It was probably George Orwell who pointed out that totalitarians want to control the past as much as they control the future and so history has to be re-written. Important figures at one time may have to be airbrushed out of group photographs when they fall from favour with some later regime. In addition there must be no criticism of failures on the way to the goal, otherwise people may doubt the very goals themselves and the people may cease to have confidence in the leadership.

The rational alternative is piecemeal change and reform. People who adopt this method may or may not have a complete blueprint of society in mind, and they may be open-minded about the amount of progress that can be achieved. The moral principles proposed in Chapter 5 - minimise suffering rather than maximise happiness, promote tolerance and avoid tyranny - fit like a glove with piecemeal reform, and with democratic government. Most people can agree on concrete steps to address suffering and the problems of people in need, whereas there are likely to be many conflicting views on the way that happiness should be sought.

While piecemeal reform fits democracy, Utopian reform demands a dictatorship, and a harsh and uncompromising one to boot. However the dictator, even one who is benevolent, will have great difficulty finding out from his sycophantic courtiers whether the effects of his policies match his intentions.

Two misunderstandings of piecemeal reform need to be corrected. First of all, the piecemeal reformer does not have to be pessimistic or negative about the prospects for major improvements. Many things have been realized in the western democracies which were once dogmatically declared to be unrealizable, for instance a degree of civil peace and the reduction of the ranks of the suffering poor to a very small proportion of the population.

Second, the piecemeal reformer is not restricted to petty, trivial or small scale experiments, such as reforms of a single village. The reformer will mostly be concerned with social institutions which extend throughout the whole of society, like the legal system and taxation and trade policy.

Chapter 10: The Open Society

In this chapter Popper used the term "open society" to mean a society in which people have an opportunity to make personal decisions and the "closed society" is a magical or tribal or collectivist society. The chapter begins with Popper's quest for some mitigating factor that might have been missing from his analysis of Plato as a totalitarian party-politician. He identified this in Plato's genuine hatred of tyranny and his desire to make the people happy by relieving the strain of social and political change. Popper depicted the origin of western civilisation in the Greek states as a transition from a closed or tribal society in the direction of an open society. This transition caused strain and distress which Popper called the "strain of civilisation", a problem that is liable to intensify at any time of social or political dislocation.

Sections II and III examine the conditions in the Greek states round about the sixth century BC, leading up to the Peloponnesian War between Athens and Sparta, and the bitter and destructive divisions between democrats and others in Athens itself.

Section IV is an idealized account of the aspirations of Pericles and the Great Generation of Athenian democrats. Section V describes the contribution that the historical Socrates made to the debate on political principles in Athens ending in his trial and his death sentence.

Sections VI to VIII address the political events after the death of Socrates with some speculation about the internal tensions in Plato's mind as he drifted from the principles of the historical Socrates and transformed the Socrates of the later into dialogues into a mouthpiece for his own program to restore the wholeness and stability of the state.

Plato and the happiness of the people

Popper felt that something was missing from his interpretation of Plato as a totalitarian party-politician who did not succeed in his immediate efforts but put in place a powerful and convincing body of anti-democratic and anti-individualistic ideas. For centuries those ideas have undermined the efforts of democratic social reformers and promoted collectivist programs. After a largely unsuccessful search for evidence to refute that interpretation Popper concluded that Plato was seriously opposed to tyranny and he really cared about the happiness of the people.

> The one point in which I felt that my search for a refutation had succeeded concerned Plato's hatred of tyranny...I am ready to grant his fundamental benevolence. I also grant that he was right, to a limited extent, in the sociological analysis on which he based his promise of happiness. (170)

This points up the danger of adopting the greatest happiness as a major guiding principle for social reform, at the expense of freedom. Aldous Huxley made this point in his futuristic nightmare *Brave New World* where the people lived in an indolent drug-induced state of contentment.

Closed and open societies

One of Popper's signature ideas is the contrast between the open and closed or tribal society. These need to be seen as ideal types which never occur in pure forms but the contrast is helpful to explain Popper's historical account. Popper's use of these terms is practically the same as that advanced by the poet W. H. Auden in "Criticism in a mass society".

1. There are two types of society: closed societies and open.

2. All human societies begin by being of the closed type, but, except when they have stagnated or died, they have always evolved toward an ever more and more open type.

3. Up until the industrial revolution this evolution was so gradual as hardly to be perceptible within the lifespan of an individual. The evolutionary process is complicated by the fact that different sections of the community progress towards the open society at different speeds. At any given point in history there are classes for whom economic, political and cultural advantages make society relatively open, and vice versa, those for whom similar disadvantages make it relatively closed. No human community of course has ever been completely closed, and none probably will ever be completely open, but from the researches of anthropologists and historians, we can construct a Platonic idea of both. (Auden, 1941)

The strain of civilisation and the fear of freedom

Popper described what he called the "strain of civilization", that is, the experience of tension or uneasiness which is likely to arise from rapid or unpredictable social change, or the transition from a more or less protected situation at home or at school to the more challenging environment of the world outside.

As soon as one is alert to the strain of civilisation it can be seen as a recurring motif in historical and sociological studies, although it is not usually articulated in a robust theory which provides both an explanation and some pointers for a rational response. Children of the sixties and seventies may recall a book by Erich Fromm called *The Fear of Freedom* which was a psychological explanation of the appeal of fascism, couched in Marxist and Freudian terms.

The theory of the strain of civilization could have provided a framework for subsequent work on the problems of social change and multicultural societies, however it has never, to my knowledge, been used by any well-known or influential anthropologist, historian or sociologist. This may reflect the dominance of people in those professions who were scandalized by Popper's treatment of Plato and Marx, or it may be, as the late Roger Sandall suggested in personal communication, that it became politically incorrect in progressive circles to talk about tribal societies in any way that implied that they are inferior to western civilization.

Plato's betrayal of Socrates and the Great Generation

After sketching the theory of tribal transition and the strain of civilisation, Popper returned to the causes and consequences of the breakdown of tribalism and isolationism in the Greek states, leading to a class war and a war between Greece and Sparta, the two leading cities of Greece. In this story, Popper's heroes are Socrates and the Great Generation, led by Pericles, a generation inspired by a new faith in reason, freedom and the brotherhood of all men. Pericles formulated the principle of equality before the law and of political individualism, and Herodotus was welcomed in Pericles' city as a historian who admired these principles.

Socrates was not a political leader or a theorist of the open society. He was a critic, (a friendly critic) of democracy. Popper insisted that democracy needs critics to press for improvements, and they should not be seen as hostile to democracy, indeed he suggested that democrats who do not see the difference between a friendly and a hostile criticism of democracy are themselves imbued with the totalitarian spirit.

Chapter 11: The Aristotelian Roots of Hegelianism

This chapter has three sections after a short introduction. Section I contains a brief sketch of Aristotle's political philosophy and some other aspects of his work. Section II is an extended critique of the methodology and epistemology which involves the quest for true definitions and detailed conceptual analysis or "explication" which Popper labelled essentialism. The notes attached to this section contain full-fledged essays on a range of topics, including Wittgenstein's earlier philosophy. Section III consists of brief notes on some episodes in the ancient battle between authoritarian rule and the relatively democratic spirit of Pericles and the Great Generation of Athens.

It is helpful to recall that Popper's critique of Plato and Aristotle was not designed to belittle their achievements but to draw attention to elements of their work which undermine effective thought and action in the social sciences and in politics. It was not supposed to be a "fair appraisal" of their achievements (which he valued highly) but an attempt to eliminate error.

Section I describes Aristotle's ambivalent attitude to democracy and his recognition of the need to compromise with a system that he found distasteful. He endorsed the Platonic idea that some men are slaves by nature and his theory of the best state combines elements of Platonic aristocracy, feudalism and some elements of democracy. He taught that some men are free by nature and others are slaves by nature, and for the latter, slavery is fitting and just. Popper commented that for Aristotle the working classes do not rule and the ruling classes do not work, nor earn any money, a tradition that came down to the British class system of modern times. It seems that hunting and war have often been the major hobbies of the ruling classes. The distinction between amateur and professional cricketers in England was another amusing illustration of this of attitude which was replicated in the Olympic games and some other sports including tennis and upper-class rugby until recent times.

The final cause

One of Aristotle's legacies is the idea of the Final Cause which is associated with his biological interests and also with the notion of action with a purpose (teleology). Modern science has shed the idea of teleology in nature, including biology; so we appreciate that the plant roots do not deliberately grow towards the water. Roots which happen to grow towards water, and reach it, may live while those which grow in the "wrong" direction will die.

Aristotle was important for Popper's criticism of historical determinism because Hegel took up the Aristotelian notion that movement, change or evolution reveal the essence of the object. Thus it follows that social events can only be understood by applying the historical method in order to penetrate beneath the surface of things to locate their hidden essence.

Essentialism

Popper noted that the problem of definitions and the meaning of terms does not directly bear upon historicism but it has caused confusion and impeded effective criticism of unhelpful ideas. The second section of Chapter 11 is a critique of the preoccupation with the definition of terms and the explication of concepts which Popper labelled essentialism. The issue emerged from the ancient problem of universals, that is, the question of whether there are general categories of things over and above the individual instances of things that we observe. Popper was writing about this in section 10 of *The Poverty of Historicism* and he found that his historical notes on the problem kept growing until he put aside the manuscript of *The Poverty* and wrote *The Open Society and Its Enemies* instead.

People who habitually address social issues with an imaginative and critical attitude to alternative policies and their likely outcomes will not benefit much from the critique of verbalism and conceptual analysis. However they may have friends or relations who have picked up bad habits and these people may need professional help.

In a nutshell, essentialism claims that true belief (knowledge) results from either (a) an intuitive grasp of the essence of things, or (b) clarification or explication of the concept of the (various) things.

> Like Plato, Aristotle believed that we obtain all knowledge ultimately by an intuitive grasp of the essences of things. 'We can know a thing only by knowing its essence', Aristotle writes, and 'to know a thing is to know its essence'. A basic premise is, according to him, nothing but a statement describing the essence of a thing. But such a statement is just what he calls a definition. Thus all 'basic premises of proofs' are definitions. (Vol. ii, 10)

Hence the fundamental problem in the theory of knowledge and education is to get hold of the correct definitions or basic premises. Aristotle followed Plato with rather more emphasis on the role of observation in place of Plato's intellectual intuition of the Ideal Forms but in the end he relied heavily on a mental or intellectual faculty which enables us to grasp the essences of things.

Popper ended the chapter with a brief critique of the idea that we have a faculty of intellectual intuition which enables us to visualize essences and recognize which definition is the correct one. Popper willingly conceded that we possess something which may be described as intellectual intuition and this accounts for the experience of understanding an idea or a process such as multiplication in arithmetic. That process of insight and understanding can be very powerful and there are countless intellectual experiences of that kind but none of them constitute a warrant for the truth of the insight although it sometimes comes as a revelation!

He also described how natural scientists have avoided prolonged verbal disputes by refusing to spend a lot of time on definitions and ensuring that our statements never depend too much on the meaning of the words. He used the terms "sand-dune" and "wind" to make the point: they are vague (when does a sand hill become a dune?).

> However, for many of the geologist's purposes, these terms are quite sufficiently precise; and for other purposes, when a higher degree of differentiation is needed, he can always say 'dunes between 4 and 30 feet high' or 'wind of a velocity of between 20 and 40 miles an hour'. (Vol. ii, 19)

Chapter 12 Hegel and The New Tribalism

Popper could not take Hegel seriously as a major thinker although he regarded him as a devastating influence on German philosophy and intellectual life at large. Popper's views have attracted criticism from admirers of Hegel but I have not attempted to offer a commentary.

Chapter 13: Sociological Determinism

This chapter has only eight pages, starting with a lunge at the enemies of the open society who penetrated the humanitarian under cover of various Trojan horses such as Plato's idea of (collective) justice, the Christian authoritarianism of the middle ages, and Rousseau's theory of the general will.

Popper did not want to dwell on the similarities between Marxism and its fascist counterpart despite their similar intellectual origin because he regarded Marx and Marxism as genuinely humanitarian (at their best) and Marx himself attempted to apply rational methods to social problems. However: "The value of this attempt is impaired by the fact that it was, as I shall try to show, largely unsuccessful."(Vol. ii, 81) Surprisingly, Popper allowed that statement to stand in revised editions of the book even after he read Schwarzchild's book on Marx, *The Red Prussian*, and he stated that the evidence demonstrated that Marx "was less of a humanitarian and a lover of freedom, than he is made to appear in my book" (Vol. ii, 396). Popper described Marx's practical interest in social science to further the cause of human liberation, but this interest did not extend to practical short-term reforms and so he misled countless people into thinking that historical prophecy is the scientific way to engage with social problems.

> Marx is responsible for the devastating influence of the historicist method of thought within the ranks of those who wish to advance the cause of the open society...The vast economic researches of Marx did not even touch the problems of a constructive economic policy, for example, economic planning. (Vol. ii, 82-83)

In other words Marx had no theory of social reform, so what does that make of his vast economic researches? The vast researches largely consisted of reading secondary sources that were written to indict the social system without taking account of the improvements that were happening while they should have been getting worse, according to Marx.

One of the responses to criticism is to retreat to the position that Marxism is primarily a method of analysis rather than a doctrine, so that even if some of his predictions are refuted, like the predictions of revolution, the method remains intact. Popper was prepared to accept that Marxism is fundamentally a method and he examined the method and see how helpful it really is.

Chapter 14: The Autonomy of Sociology

This chapter contains an early statement of Popper's ideas on explanation in the social sciences by "situational analysis" which he regarded as the standard procedure in neoclassical microeconomics. He named Marx as a pioneer in this approach because he rejected the idea that motives or psychological factors provide an adequate explanation of socioeconomic structures and historical events.

The chapter opens with an example to demonstrate Marx's view on the primacy of social existence over consciousness. This is the apparently universal fear of snakes.

> This aversion has a greater semblance of being instinctive or "natural" in that it is exhibited not only by men but also by all anthropoid apes and by most monkeys as well. But experiments seem to indicate that this fear is conventional. It appears to be a product of education, not only in the human race but also for instance in chimpanzees, since both young children and young chimpanzees who have not been taught to fear snakes do not exhibit the alleged instinct. (Vol. ii, 89-90)

So it seems that social intervention and learning are required to produce what might be regarded as a universal psychological trait. He referred to the concise formulation of Marx's opposition to psychologism, (the reduction of all laws of social life to the psychological laws of human nature) "It is not the consciousness of man that determines his existence—rather, it is his social existence that determines his consciousness."

Institutions of various kinds and also traditions are important aspects of the situation. In his approach to traditions and institutions Popper noted that these things are man-made "in a certain sense" with some important qualifications; for example they are not usually made by conscious design although a great deal of this has been attempted in the last two centuries. One of Popper's slogans is "Only a minority of social institutions are consciously designed, while the vast majority have just 'grown', as the undesigned results of human actions." That was "in the air" in Vienna due to the influence of Carl Menger and the Austrian school of economics, following Adam Smith and the Scottish political economists.

Chapter 15: Economic Historicism

The major points which Popper advanced in this chapter are (1) Marx was not a Vulgar Marxist, (2) Marx was not a simple-minded materialist and (3) the "fundamental importance" of economic analysis can be overdone.

Popper debunked the "Vulgar Marxist" idea that Marx can be seen as a rival of Freud and Adler to penetrate to the hidden springs of human motivation. Marx sometimes spoke of psychological phenomena like greed and the profit motive, but he did not use them as explanations, rather they were symptoms of the corrupting influence of the social system; they were effects rather than causes.

The chapter contains three sections. The first two examine Marx's economic historicism by drawing a contrast with Mill's resort to psychological explanations of social phenomena, especially the life of the mind. The third section is critical of the tendency to make too much out of the idea that the economic and material base are all-important to explain the function of social institutions and their historical development.

Materialism and the life of the mind

As a poet in his youth and an educated member of the cultured bourgeoisie, Marx did not denigrate things of the mind, even when he depicted the products of mind as part of the superstructure rather than the base of things.

> There is a well-known passage in Capital, where Marx says that 'in Hegel's writing, dialectics stands on its head; one must turn it the right way up again …' Its tendency is clear. Marx wished to show that the head, i.e. human thought, is not itself the basis of human life but rather a kind of superstructure, on a physical basis. (Vol. ii, 102)

As to the material part of the dualism, social science is practically identical with scientific history, and that is supposed to explore the laws of development in our exchange of matter with nature – the conditions of production.

Critique – two aspects of historical materialism

Moving on to criticism, Popper distinguished two different aspects, first, historicism, the claim that the realm of social sciences coincides with that of the historical or evolutionary method, and especially with historical prophecy. The second aspect is economism or "materialism", i.e. the claim that the economic organization of society is fundamental for all social institutions and especially for their historical development. Popper dismissed the first claim and agreed with the second provided that the term 'fundamental' is not taken too seriously.

Chapter 16: The Classes

The critique of Marx's theory of the classes follows the lines taken up in the last chapter. The formula "all history is a history of class struggle" is valuable as a reminder to look into the part played by class struggle in power politics as well as in other developments. But dissention within the Marxian classes is at least as important as the conflict between the classes. Consequently the Marxist theory of classes is a dangerous over-simplification. An example is the interpretation of WW1 (especially by

German Marxists) as a struggle between the "have-not" Central Powers and an alliance of conservative or "have" countries.

> On the other hand, his attempt to use what may be called the "logic of the class situation" to explain the working of the institutions of the industrial system seems to me admirable in spite of certain exaggerations and the neglect of some important aspects of the situation; admirable, at least, as a sociological analysis of that stage of the industrial system which Marx has mainly in mind: the system of "unrestrained capitalism" (as I shall call it) of one hundred years ago. (Vol. ii, 117)

Increasing productivity and exploitation of the workers

For Popper the most important function of the class conflict theory is to explain the increase in productivity which is an integral part of Marx's story to account for the revolution and the advent of freedom under socialism. Traditional history, mostly concerned with military power and the conflict of nations, did not shed any light on productivity and progress in agriculture and industry. Since Popper wrote in the 1940s there has been a great deal of work on that theme. A striking example is Terence Kealey in *The Economic Laws of Scientific Research*, especially Chapter 5 on the agricultural revolution.

Popper continued his critique of Mill and psychological explanations because he did not accept the idea that class interest is a psychological phenomenon. He argued that Marx, some of the time, pursued an institutional analysis (rejecting psychologism) and in this respect Popper regarded him as an important pioneer of sociological analysis. Marx argued that the ruling capitalists were trapped in the system just as much as the workers. This is a corrective to the moralistic view that the rulers should have been kinder; on this deterministic account they had no alternative.

Chapter 17: The Legal and Social System

This chapter could be called "The Legal, Political and Social System". Popper described it as probably the most crucial point in his criticism of

Marxism; it is Marx's theory of the state and as strange as it may seem, of the impotence of politics.

Section I describes the theory of the state. Section II describes the "grim reality" of social conditions for the workers at the time that Marx was working in England. Section III contains Popper's arguments on the need to use political power to control economic power (contra the Marxian doctrine of the impotence of politics).

Section IV (the central point) concerns the difference between historical prediction and rational social engineering. Section V defends the importance of "formal freedom" against radical critics who claim that freedom under the rule of law is not real freedom as long as there is inequality because some people are poor.

Section VI notes how Marx and his followers failed to pay attention to the need to control political power. Section VII is about the need to use impartial rules rather than discretionary orders from politicians and bureaucrats for fair and effective public administration.

The theory of the state

Marx's theory of the state is presented by combining the results chapters 15 and 16. The legal and political system—the system of legal institutions enforced by the state— is understood as one of the superstructures erected upon (and expressing) the actual productive forces of the economic system.

"Political power, properly so called,' says the Manifesto, 'is merely the organized power of one class for oppressing the other."

This view of the state and the political system is partly a (rational) institutional analysis and partly an (irrefutable) essentialist theory. The essentialist approach starts with the question "What is the state?" instead of the realistic reformer's question, cast in the language of political proposals - "What functions do we want the state to perform?"

The most important (and dangerous) outcome of the Marxist analysis is that legal and political institutions can never be of primary importance and the Marxist theory of politics was fatally flawed because it did not warn Marxists or socialists to be alert to abuses of power (other than economic power) and the need for institutional checks and balances on all forms of power.

Exploitation

While Popper considered that the Marxist methodology and program were fatally flawed, he conceded that Marx was correct in his appraisal of the "grim and depressing experience" of the "most shameless and cruel exploitation" that prevailed at the time. This is not a strong part of Popper's analysis because the record reveals that the workers were moving ahead (from a low base) as a result of the industrial revolution and the movement of workers from farms to factories. Hutt's paper on the misrepresentation of the conditions of children working in the cotton mills is an important corrective to the account that became standard in the literature under the influence of Marxist and labour-oriented historians such as the Webbs (Hutt, 1951).

The political control of economic power

Popper did not accept Marx's view that the political and institutional framework could not be reformed to obtain improvements, so a full-scale social revolution would be required. He noted the equally radical alternative point of view.

> Or are we to believe the defenders of an unrestrained 'capitalist' system who emphasize (rightly, I think) the tremendous benefit to be derived from the mechanism of free markets, and who conclude from this that a truly free labour market would be of the greatest benefit to all concerned? (Vol. ii, 124)

Despite his friendship with Hayek and the respect he held for Hayek's ideas in general Popper did not accept the free market approach to the labour market and he thought that various forms of state intervention would be required to protect the workers from exploitation.

The central point of the analysis

For Popper the central part of his argument with Marx concerns the efficacy of political power and the role of non-violent institutional reform. This is where Marxist ideas about practical reforms and public administration reveal the significance of the clash between historicism and social engineering, and the way this clash created problems for the friends of freedom and the open society.

Popper concluded that Marx's own theory rules out progress by peaceful political changes such as legal reforms. Politics can only shorten and lessen the birth pangs of the new society.

> This, I think, is an extremely poor political programme, and its poverty is a consequence of the third-rate place which it attributes to political power in the hierarchy of powers...the real power lies in the evolution of machinery; next in importance is the system of economic class-relationships; and the least important influence is that of politics. (Vol. ii, 125-6)

In contrast Popper considered political power as fundamental and he envisaged a comprehensive legislative program to control economic power – laws to limit the working day, insurance for various form of disability, unemployment, old age. However Marx derided reformers on the ground that they were utopian and the business of historical science was to make predictions, not to guide interventions. And so Marx's theories tended to block the development of helpful reforms and the Marxists did not see the need to control political power after the revolution or to be alarmed at the prospect of the "dictatorship of the proletariat".

The importance of "formal freedom"

Having discovered the importance of economic power it is not surprising that Marx made too much of it. Economic power is everywhere, it can buy anything.

> Their argument runs: he who has the money has the power; for if necessary, he can buy guns and even gangsters. But this is a

roundabout argument. In fact, it contains an admission that the man who has the gun has the power. And if he who has the gun becomes aware of this, then it may not be long until he has both the gun and the money. (Vol. ii, 127)

The notion that economic power is at the root of all evil needs to be replaced by the appreciation of the dangers of any form of power, especially when it is centralized.

The danger of intervention

Popper warned that any kind of economic intervention, even the limited and piecemeal kind that he advocated, would increase the power of the state. He warned that freedom is at stake if we relax our watchfulness. We must maintain controls on the power of the state as it expands its functions.

In addition to the "paradox of freedom" which Popper described in Chapter 7, there is also a paradox of state planning. "If we plan too much, if we give too much power to the state, then freedom will be lost, and that will be the end of planning." (Vol. ii, 130).

This takes us back to the case for piecemeal, and against Utopian social engineering and to the proposal to target concrete evils instead of pinning our hopes on the establishment of some ideal good.

Persons and institutions: rules and orders

The remainder of the chapter is concerned with the kind of legislative and administrative arrangements that are required for the state to intervene without allowing dangerous discretionary powers to be assumed by politicians or officials. Possibly influenced by correspondence with Hayek, Popper proposed that state intervention should proceed by way of protective laws and a legal framework instead of empowering organs or agents of the state to act as they see fit to achieve the ends laid down by the rulers at the time.

The introduction of piecemeal reforms permits the application of the method of trial and error to make adjustments in the light of experience in slowly changing the permanent legal framework. In contrast discretionary decisions by politicians and civil servants are short-term, often reflexive and opportunistic, and are not usually subjected to public discussion and scrutiny before they are launched.

The legal framework should be designed to be understandable and predictable, providing a degree of certainty and security in social life. So in Popper's view, when the framework is altered, allowances should be made during a transitional period for those individuals who have laid their plans in the expectation of its constancy. The situation is radically different when changes are introduced in the form of personal intervention by the rulers. National emergencies calling for special efforts to address clearly defined crises may be exceptions to the rule of piecemeal reform of the framework. However if direct intervention becomes the rule then the result will be ever-increasing unpredictability and insecurity (the modern phrase is regime uncertainty). People will come to fear that events are being driven by powers "behind the scenes", fuelling conspiracy theories of society "with all its consequences – heresy hunts, national, social and class hostility." (vol. 2, 133).

Chapter 18: The Coming of Socialism

The next three chapters (18, 19 and 20) test the coherence of the chain of predictions for the coming of socialism following the revolution. Popper identified three steps in the argument.

1. The capitalist system generates increased productivity, greater inequality between the rich and the poor, and increasing misery for the workers.

2. Eventually only two classes are left and the tension between them will precipitate the revolution.

3. The classless society of socialism will emerge.

In this chapter Popper examined (3), the case for the emergence of the classless society after the revolution and he found that there were other and more likely outcomes. In the next chapter he went back in the chain of argument to see if step 2 followed from step 1. In chapter 20 he critically examined the first step of the argument, especially the claim of increasing misery of the workers.

Granting the first two steps, the question at this stage is: can we assume that a classless society will emerge from a battle between the bourgeoisie and the proletariat after these are the only two classes left and the increasing misery of the workers has driven them to desperation? In Popper's view there was no assurance that the workers' victory must lead to a classless society because classes are not like individuals and whatever unity they might manage to achieve during a "class war" would be most unlikely to survive the end of the conflict with the "class enemy".

Popper thought that the most likely development would be that the winners of the battle, the revolutionary leaders who survived the war and the various purges, with their close associates, would form a New Class, a kind of new aristocracy or bureaucracy.

> And it seems likely enough that they will be able to make fullest use of the revolutionary ideology if at the same time they exploit the fear of counter-revolutionary developments. In this way, the revolutionary ideology will serve them for apologetic purposes: it will serve them both as a vindication of the use they make of their power, and as a means of stabilizing it; in short, as a new 'opium for the people'." (Vol. ii, 138)

Chapter 19: The Social Revolution

This chapter contains six sections, and a lot of arguments are packed into 15 pages.

Section I treats the second step of Marx's prophetic argument, specifically the prediction that the class war will end in a battle between the bourgeoisie and the proletariat (the last classes standing.)

Section II pursues the question, does the Marxist revolution have to be violent? Section III compares the radical and moderate Marxist attitudes to revolutionary violence. Section IV explores the ambiguity of Marxist attitudes towards violence and the legitimacy of opposition parties.

Section V outlines the various ways that Marxist rhetoric undermined democracy and Section VI describes how that played out in practice, opening the way for fascism.

The bourgeoisie vs the proletariat

Marx wrote "Each capitalist lays many of his fellows low", and so the lower strata of the middle class, the small tradesmen, shopkeepers, and retired tradesmen, the handicraftsmen and the peasants, will all sink into the proletariat.

Popper thought that there was some truth in that account, especially so far as handicrafts and some farm workers are concerned but it neglected the rise of new occupations and trades in emerging industries. Also there was no guarantee that the rural proles and others who might be displaced would actually align their interests with the urban factory workers. For the purpose of the argument at this stage, Popper conceded the assumption of increasing misery of the masses but he argued that even this would not guarantee the solidarity of the oppressed.

> Thus, as opposed to Marx's prophecy which insists that there must develop a neat division between two classes, we find that on his own assumptions, the following class structure may possibly develop: (1) bourgeoisie, (2) big landed proprietors, (3) other landowners, (4) rural workers, (5) new middle class, (6) industrial workers, (7) rabble proletariat. (Any other combination of these classes may, of course, develop too.) And we find, furthermore, that such a development may possibly undermine the unity of (6).

We can say, therefore, that the first conclusion of the second step in Marx's argument does not follow. (Vol. ii, 148)

Violence and the social revolution

For Popper the prophecy of a possibly violent revolution is possibly the most harmful element in Marxism from the point of view of practical politics and protecting freedom and democracy. It is likely that Marx anticipated civil war between the classes on the way to socialism and this was not really such a bad thing because on his analysis social life before the revolution is inherently violent and the class war claims victims every day. Popper suggested that for Marx, "What really matters is the result, socialism. To achieve this result is the essential characteristic of the social revolution." (vol. 2, 149) For Popper it was apparent from some of Marx's rhetoric that he was not concerned about the prospect of mayhem and murder, just as long as the bourgeoisie lost.

Popper raised some political and moral issues related to the prophecy of revolution and the probable need for this to be violent. He noted the importance of the rhetoric of violence, so in some respects the actual use of violence is less important than the intention which can be used to intimidate opponents.

> If a man is determined to use violence in order to achieve his aims, then we may say that to all intents and purposes he adopts a violent attitude, whether or not violence is actually used in a particular case. (Vol. ii, 150)

Rules on the use of violence by people of good will

A little-appreciated part of Popper's thinking is what Jarvie called his "social turn" to be alert to the pervasive influence of conventions and "rules of the game" (Jarvie, 2001). We need to become aware of rules and conventions, to appreciate their importance and to critically examine alternatives to improve the system, whether the focus is scientific research or political practice or running a household (sharing the chores).

Popper followed some medieval and Renaissance Christian thinkers who taught that tyrannicide could be justified (also just wars). In a situation where there is no other way to get rid of a tyrant then a violent revolution to achieve regime change may be justified. But he went on to write that any such revolution should have as its only aim the establishment of a democracy. And by democracy he did not mean something as vague as "the rule of the people" or "the rule of the majority", but a set of institutions (such as general elections) which permit public control of the rulers.

People who are not outright pacifists have to be prepared to condone certain kinds of violent behaviour by themselves or by their representatives (the army and police). The vital questions concern the circumstances and the kind of violence to be used. Later in this chapter he offered some rules for the regulation and control of violence in democracies, that is by peace-loving people of good will.

One kind of violence which he condoned in principle is that required to remove a tyranny if no other means are available. That is a dangerous move if it is not quickly effective because the prolonged use of violence will undermine the dispassionate rule of reason, and possibly deliver not freedom but the rule of the strong man and his cronies.

Radicals and moderates

Popper examined the ambivalent attitude towards violence which was fostered by both the radical and moderate wings of the Marxist movement, essentially the communist and social democrat parties as they existed in Europe between WW1 and WW2. Sometimes the issue was pushed aside because the Marxist in his capacity as a scientist was concerned with predictions and not moral positions.

The radical wing had no qualms about a violent revolution because on the Marxist account all class rule is necessarily a dictatorship, i.e. a tyranny and hence fair game for violence. The moderate wing insisted that some advances towards democracy can be made under the existing regime and so the social revolution might occur by way of peaceful and gradual reforms.

> But even this moderate wing insists that such a peaceful development is uncertain; it points out that it is the bourgeoisie which is likely to resort to force, if faced with the prospect of being defeated by the workers on the democratic battlefield; and it contends that in this case the workers would be justified in retaliating, and in establishing their rule by violent means. Both wings claim to represent the true Marxism of Marx, and in a way, both are right." [due to the ambiguity in his formulations and changes in his position over his lifetime] (Vol. ii, 153)

The radical position is more consistent with the apocalyptic tone of the prophecies. From the radical or hardline point of view, capitalism has to be eliminated by violence if it is to be eliminated at all. In contrast the moderate position appeared to accept the possibility of non-violent expropriation of the capitalists by capturing the democratic process, a prospect that was realistic in England by the time Marx died.

Two ambiguities: violence and the conquest of power

In this section and the next Popper described how the Marxists tended to undermine democracy by their ambiguity towards violence and the conquest of power. Peace and freedom loving Marxists have not been helped by the more apocalyptic and bloodthirsty passages of Marx, nor by the irrational worship of violence by the revolutionaries in the adversary culture.

The essentialist theory of the state is also a major problem – the theory that the state is essentially a class tyranny. This makes it very hard for reasonable Marxists to adopt the language of political proposals to work towards a functioning democracy with proposals to achieve good government with a protective state, the rule of law and the like.

Popper was especially critical of the tactical doctrine promulgated by Engels along the lines that Marxists would like to achieve a peaceful and democratic development towards socialism, but as political realists they expected the bourgeoisie to give up democracy if the workers become the majority. In that event Marxists must be prepared to fight to gain political power and the workers should be prepared for that possibility. This resulted in persistent talk of violence, especially by radical and romantic elements of the movement which made the working of democracy impossible wherever the ambivalent rhetoric of revolution was adopted by a major political party. Here Popper adopted the "rules of the game" approach to suggest that democracy can work only if the main parties are alert to the danger of power without checks and balances and also maintain standards of public debate and respect for free speech.

He suggested that democracy cannot be usefully defined as the rule of the majority, because a majority might rule in a tyrannical way. For example the majority might decide that only a small minority of the rich should pay income tax. The really important requirement is the limitation of the powers of the rulers.

> ...and the criterion of a democracy is this: In a democracy, the rulers—that is to say, the government—can be dismissed by the ruled without bloodshed. Thus if the men in power do not safeguard those institutions which secure to the minority the possibility of working for a peaceful change, then their rule is a tyranny. (Vol. ii, 160)

Institutions are required to protect minorities although that protection should not extend to unlimited tolerance of people who are themselves intolerant or use violence to attack democracy. Vigilance is required to be alert to antidemocratic tendencies among the people as well as among the rulers.

> Democracy provides an invaluable battle-ground for any reasonable reform, since it permits reform without violence. But if the preservation of democracy is not made the first consideration in any particular battle fought out on this battle-ground, then the latent anti-democratic tendencies which are always present may bring about a breakdown of democracy. (Vol. ii, 160-61)

Popper was concerned that Marxists too often encouraged the workers to be suspicious of democracy, quoting Engels "In reality the state is nothing more than a machine for the oppression of one class by another, and this holds for a democratic republic no less than for a monarchy." (Vol. ii, 161). The result of this is to blame democracy for problems and evils as though democracy is supposed to be a magic cure-all that automatically prevents bad things from happening. In reality democracy is a framework for effective administration and more or less reasonable discussion of reforms. The Engels approach means teaching the people to consider the state not as theirs, but as belonging to the rulers, and to claim that the only one way to improve things is the complete conquest of power (winner take all).

> And against the Manifesto which says ambiguously: 'The first step in the revolution of the working class is to raise the proletariat to the position of the ruling class—to win the battle of democracy', I assert that if this is accepted as the first step, then the battle of democracy will be lost. (Vol. ii, 162)

The remainder of the chapter sketched some of the ways that the Marxists doctrines played out in practical politics, culminating in the rise and triumph of fascism. While the social democrats lacked the will to resist effectively, the communists managed to convince themselves that there was no need to resist (ultimately) because fascism represented the last gasp of capitalism and it should be allowed to run its course.

Chapter 20: Capitalism and its Fate

This chapter steps back to the first of the three stages in the prediction, namely the inevitability of increasing exploitation and misery of the workers. Section I is a sketch of the premises of Marx's prophecy, the laws of capitalist production and accumulation, and the conclusion, namely the law of increasing wealth (on one side) and misery (on the other).

Four sections are devoted to some subsidiary assumptions that are required for the argument followed by two sections of critical analysis.

Most of the three volumes of *Capital* (over 2000 pages) are devoted to the inner contradictions of capitalism, supported by statistics on the system at the time, which Popper called unrestrained capitalism. These represent the first step in the chain of events that leads to the socialist revolution. As Lenin put it: Marx deduces the inevitability of the transformation of capitalist society into socialism wholly and exclusively from the economic law of the movement of contemporary society.

Popper addressed the three basic assumptions about the outcome of capitalistic competition (1) increasing productivity, (2) accumulation of the means of production (and wealth) and (3) increasing misery of the workers.

He accepted (1) without dispute. He did not accept (2) as inevitable due to the possibility of various forms of intervention. He considered (3) as the most important prophecy especially as he was concerned with the minimizing suffering as a prime objective of public policy.

Three different trends of thought may be distinguished in Marx's attempts to establish the "increasing misery" prophecy. These are the theory of value, surplus population and the trade cycle.

The theory of value

Since the marginal revolution in economics in the 1870s the labor theory of value would appear to have little interest but Popper did a highly nuanced appraisal of it. One wonders how much Colin Simkin contributed; he was the young economist who Popper befriended in Christchurch and recruited to assist with discussion and checking the English. Popper concluded that Marx's value theory did not suffice to explain exploitation, but it is not essential.

Surplus population

Popper was prepared to put aside Marx's labour theory of value and his theory of surplus value to focus on the pressure exerted on wages by a the surplus population of the chronically unemployed. He had no doubt that the surplus population would ensure something like starvation wages for the workers. However he considered that Marx's analysis was defective because he did not envisage the kind of interventions that would enable the workers to combine and improve their conditions.

The trade cycle

On Popper's view Marx's analysis of the trade cycle rests very largely upon the assumption (which Popper regarded as a fact) that a surplus population actually existed at his time and so the workers were in no position to press for better conditions. But it is likely that the "fact" of surplus population is on a par with the "fact" of exploitation. It is not explained because it did not exist in the form that was assumed by Marx. The notion of surplus population in Britain is problematic. When child labour ceased under the factory legislation, Irish labourers turned up to take the places of the children which suggests that there was not a surplus population of workers looking for employment in Britain at the time.

The surplus population is central to Marx's theory of the trade cycle, of depressions, the resulting misery and the prophecy of the crash of the capitalist system. Popper did not attempt a detailed analysis of Marx's theory of the trade cycle because he admitted that he did not know enough about the issues. On advice from Colin Simkin (at that stage something of a Keynesian and a great admirer of the Scandinavian countries) he mentioned the possibility of counter-cyclic intervention which of course was something that Marx did not know about.

Popper came near to a breakthrough in economics in the course of appraising Marx on capitalism and the "excessive" labour supply that supposedly leads to exploitation. He wrote

> What is not so clear, and not explained by Marx either, is why the supply of labour should continue to exceed the demand. For if it is so profitable to 'exploit' labour, how is it, then, that the capitalists are not forced, by competition, to try to raise their profits by employing more labour? In other words, why do they not compete

against each other in the labour market, thereby raising the
wages...It appears that the phenomena of 'exploitation' which Marx
observed were due, not, as he believed, to the mechanism of a
perfectly competitive market, but to other factors - especially to a
mixture of low productivity and imperfectly competitive markets.
(Vol. ii, 176)

Indeed, productivity increased rapidly especially with improved mobility
of people and goods with the development of canals, better roads and
the railways, so the conditions of the workers improved in defiance of
Marx's prediction of increasing misery.

The remainder of the chapter continues with "internal" criticism of the
Marx's economics, indicating that there were many potential
developments that his analysis did not envisage.

Chapter 21: An Evaluation of the Prophecy

Summing up the results of the preceding three chapters: from chapter
18 Popper concluded that there could be no guarantee that the
revolution would deliver the utopian classless society even if all the
assumptions at the previous two stages of the analysis were accurate.
From chapter 19 Popper concluded that there was no certainty about
the prophecy of the two-class society, trembling on the brink of
revolution, even if the first-stage assumption was correct. And from the
analysis in chapter 20 Popper disputed the first assumption, that the
capitalist system was bound to deliver increasing misery for the masses.

And so, in his opinion, the arguments underlying Marx's historical
prophecy are invalid and the elaborate structure of argument falls in a
heap. Popper was prepared to grant that Marx saw some things
correctly, especially the increasing productivity of the capitalist system.
Popper was also prepared to grant the accuracy of Marx's research on
the conditions of the working class and the suffering caused by
"unrestrained capitalism" but Popper's own analysis is vulnerable in
that area.

The bottom line was the failure of method, "the poverty of historicism", because there is no assurance that trends will continue even if Marx had been correct in his reading of the trends while he was at work in the British Museum.

Popper considered that the most robust parts of the Marxist prophecy concerned increasing productivity and the potentially disastrous consequences of the trade cycle (boom and bust). He did not claim to know enough to improve on Marx's analysis and he was left with the need for a theory to explain why free markets do not prevent depressions, given that the free market is supposed to adjust production and consumption to remain at least approximately in balance or tending to correct in that direction. The simple answer is that the markets were never as free as the critics of laissez faire claimed, especially towards the end of the nineteenth century as the rapid progress of the industrial revolution slowed down under the influence of increased government intervention and the rise of the welfare state, starting in Bismarck's Germany.

On the rhetorical and political impact of the prophecy, on the belief that something good would come at some point (for Marxists, after the revolution) Popper noted that Marx shared the belief of the progressive industrialists and the bourgeois of his time, that is, the belief in a law of progress. But for Popper "This naive historicist optimism is no less superstitious than a pessimistic historicism...And it is a very bad outfit for a prophet, since it must bridle historical imagination." (Vol. ii, 197).

If the Marxists had been prepared to develop what Popper called the "situational" or "institutional" analysis which Marx offered as an alternative to the psychological approach of Mill, and if they had been prepared to use this analysis to contemplate non-revolutionary social reforms, they might have achieved spectacular results as they achieved political influence. But the prophetic and pseudo-scientific character of Marxism dominated any tendency to institutional analysis and so the Marxists had no idea what was required to improve the situation wherever they came to power or managed to influence policy.

The prophetic element in Marx's creed was dominant in the minds
of his followers. It swept everything else aside, banishing the power
of cool and critical judgement and destroying the belief that by the
use of reason we may change the world. (Vol. 2, 198)

Chapter 22: The Moral Theory of Historicism

In approaching Popper's comments on the moral appeal of Marxism it is
important to recall that he was writing for a leftwing readership, like
Hayek who addressed *The Road to Serfdom* to "the socialists of the
world". This is partly because Popper was a social democrat himself and
also because practically all the intellectuals were Marxists or non-
Marxist socialists.

Given that Marxism cannot provide either reliable prophecies (nothing
can) or advice on the piecemeal reforms that might achieve desired
outcomes (Marx regarded that as Utopian) what accounts for the power
and impact of Marxism?

It seems that Marxism surfed at least three "waves" of thought. Each
was immensely powerful in its own right, and working in synergy the
combination was practically overwhelming. One of the "waves" was the
immense authority of science among educated and progressive people
150 years ago. The other was the Judeo-Christian moral imperative to
promote justice and especially to help the poor and the weak. A third
wave was the economic illiteracy of radicals and conservatives alike.
This meant that the positive function of free markets for the able-
bodied poor was never understood by enough people to resist the
manifold interventions of the state which aggravate the problems they
are supposed to ameliorate.

Near the end of the previous chapter Popper suggested that the strong
religious element in Marxism, with Marx's prophecy, inspired the
workers with a belief in their mission. In this chapter Popper outlined
the moral theory that underpinned Marxism, a somewhat paradoxical
situation because the official line on materialism and determinism at
least theoretically rule out any attempt to think our away towards an

improved social order by organized reforms. So how do we find the moral theory in Marxism?

In Popper's opinion the moral thrust of Marxism came from the method of situational analysis which tends to reveal the more remote social repercussions of current actions and institutional arrangements. The implicit (moral) message is that institutions and practices which lead to poverty and deprivation need to be reformed.

Far from promoting an explicit moral theory, Marx excoriated those moralists, especially churchmen, who were in favour of the system that he regarded as the cause of misery and exploitation. However the Marxist scheme of socio-economic determinism did not provide for autonomous moral principles. Marx's determinism was in conflict with his activism (and his implicit moralism), so the end result is that people who try to take on board the whole package of Marxism may be driven to confusion and contradiction on moral issues.

Chapter 23: The Sociology of Knowledge

Popper identified two dangerous ideas that were emerging in progressive intellectual circles during the 1930s. One was the idea of controlling social change by means of largescale central planning, the other was the theory of the social determination of scientific knowledge. One of the products of the latter impulse (some decades later) is the "strong program in the sociology of science".

This chapter signals what Ian Jarvie (2000) later called Popper's "social turn", meaning his recognition that objectivity and rationality cannot be attributed to special qualities of mind but rather to the give and take of criticism in a community.

Popper referred to the Marxist doctrine that our opinions, including our moral and scientific opinions, are determined by class interest, and more generally by the social and historical situation of our time. The main target in this chapter is Karl Mannheim. Popper objected to the tendency for sociological determinism and the sociology of knowledge to subvert the processes of critical give and take and testing that are required to identify errors and eliminate them. For a few paragraphs he played around with the idea to demonstrate what fun it could be to use apparently esoteric concepts to baffle opponents and would-be critics. Putting jokes aside he went on to explain that the emphasis on the subjective approach to knowledge (with science and knowledge depicted as processes in the mind or consciousness of individual scientists) failed to engage with the very topic of the sociology of knowledge, that is, knowledge as a public, social product.

> Considered in this [subjective] way, what we call scientific objectivity must indeed become completely incomprehensible, or even impossible; and not only in the social or political sciences, where class interests and similar hidden motives may play a part, but just as much in the natural sciences. Everyone who has an inkling of the history of the natural sciences is aware of the passionate tenacity which characterizes many of its quarrels. No amount of political partiality can influence political theories more strongly than the partiality shown by some natural scientists in favour of their intellectual offspring. (Vol. ii, 217)

The public character of scientific method comes from two aspects of scientific procedures and practices. The first is the process of (more or less) free criticism in the scientific community and the second is the way that scientists (especially natural scientists) usually try to avoid talking at cross purposes. Of course free criticism can be undermined by many factors ranging from political interference to the dominance of fads and fashions in "normal science". Similarly the obsession with conceptual refinements that Popper labelled essentialism has cramped helpful criticism and collaboration in the social sciences.

To sum up, scientific objectivity is not a result of super-human detachment and impartiality on the part of individual scientists, but a result of the public or social nature of science, an outcome of a well-functioning community. As for detachment from the world of practice, Popper insisted that practice is not the enemy of theoretical knowledge because scientists have to remain in touch with reality by testing (attempting to falsify) their theories. "Practice is not the enemy of theoretical knowledge but the most valuable incentive to it" (Vol. ii, 222).

Chapter 24: The Revolt Against Reason

"The conflict between rationalism and irrationalism has become the most important intellectual, and perhaps even moral, issue of our time." (Vol. ii, 224).

"I may be wrong and you may be right, and by an effort, we may get nearer to the truth." (Vol. ii, 225).

This is a big chapter, 26 pages, as befits a topic that has generated such a mountain of literature, much of it confused and confusing due to the numerous meanings of "reason" and "rationality" and the many and varied arguments and objections that are raised against the idea of using evidence and discussion to improve our plans and practices.

Section I spells out the kind of rationalism and rationality that Popper is prepared to defend, "an attitude that seeks to solve as many problems as possible by an appeal to clear thought and experience, rather than by an appeal to emotions and passions"(Vol. ii, 224). In case people get the idea that Popper had no time for the emotions it is helpful to note his comment that a life without emotions such as love would hardly be worth living. Further, he suggested that a deal of passion is required to make an impact in any field of human endeavour, including science.

Section II scans the long history of the conflict between rationalism and irrationalism and makes a distinction between the modest claims of "critical rationalism" and the untenable demand of "uncritical or comprehensive rationalism".

Section III explains why Popper considered that the choice is not just an intellectual matter, or a matter of taste, but a moral decision, and section IV is his moral counter-attack on irrationalism. Section V is a critique of some modern thinkers who Popper regarded as major and influential promoters of irrationalism.

For some people this is the best chapter in the book, especially those with a practical turn of mind, without much interest in the debates that go on about Popper's interpretation of Plato and Marx.

Rationalism and irrationalism

Popper used the terms reason and rationality in a broad sense to include observation, experiments, critical thinking and logic, in the way that science uses all of these things.

> Secondly, I use the word 'rationalism' in order to indicate, roughly, an attitude that seeks to solve as many problems as possible by an appeal to reason, i.e. to clear thought and experience…We could then say that rationalism is an attitude of readiness to listen to critical arguments and to learn from experience. It is fundamentally an attitude of admitting that '*I may be wrong and you may be right, and by an effort, we may get nearer to the truth.*' (Vol. ii, 225)

Listening and learning means that everyone has to be taken seriously because anyone we communicate with can be a source of information and ideas, regardless of the level of agreement between us, or our erudition or out rank and status. It establishes what Popper called the 'rational unity of mankind'. It is a highly egalitarian stance, quite unlike the Platonic idea that reason is a kind of 'faculty' that people can have and develop in different degrees.

Critical rationalism

Popper flagged the danger of taking on board "uncritical or comprehensive rationalism" which states "do not accept anything that cannot be justified by evidence and argument". This principle itself cannot be justified in the form demanded, it is paradoxical and so it exposes the uncritical rationalist to a logical beating from irrationalists who take the trouble to point out the problem. Popper based his "critical rationalism" on a decision to accept the proposal to use reason and rationality (defined above) as a general principle for problem solving and conflict resolution.

The moral dimension

Popper insisted that the choice of rationalism (in a modest from) over irrationalism is a moral decision, not just a matter of taste or an intellectual issue unconnected with the world of people and public affairs. In chapter 5 he demonstrated that evidence and arguments cannot determine fundamental moral decisions. Choices have to be made, sometimes very difficult choice and choices need to be informed by arguments and as far as possible by considering the alternative outcomes. "For only if we can visualize these consequences in a concrete and practical way, do we really know what our decision is about; otherwise we decide blindly." (Vol. ii, 232).

Consequences of irrationalism

There are some thought-provoking comments about love and imagination. Flower children of the sixties and seventies may recall the vogue of saving the world by love – a la Beatles, Erich Fromm's *The Art of Loving* etc.

> I do not overlook the fact that there are irrationalists who love mankind, and that not all forms of irrationalism engender criminality. But I hold that he who teaches that not reason but love should rule opens the way for those who rule by hate…love as such certainly does not promote impartiality. And it cannot do away with conflict either." (Vol. ii, 236)

There are other argument against the idea of a rule of love. For example loving a person means wishing to make him happy, but, as Popper pointed out, the idea of trying to make people happy by means of political reforms is a road to ruin because the most likely result will be attempts to impose some set of "higher" values on the community to "save their souls" (so they will be happy later, if not at present). In his view we have a moral duty to help people in need but not to make them happy by forcing our scale of higher values on them. He was prepared to make an exception for special efforts to interest our friends in our own passions and interests, but that depends on their freedom to ignore us or seek other company if they wish. "Thus we might say: help your enemies; assist those in distress, even if they hate you; but love only your friends." (Vol. ii, 237).

He accepted that love might move people to make an effort of imagination to comprehend the situation of people in need of help, and to take action to assist them, but he went on to argue that it is humanly impossible for us to love, or to suffer with, a great number of people; and it is not even desirable to do so because it would ultimately destroy either our ability to help or the intensity of these very emotions.

He addressed another misleading idea that is put about by enemies of reason, namely that there is some kind of affinity between imagination and emotion, so that rationalism tends to promote unimaginative dry scholasticism.

> I do not know whether such a view may have some psychological basis, and I rather doubt it. But my interests are institutional rather than psychological, and from an institutional point of view (as well as from that of method) it appears that rationalism must encourage the use of imagination because it needs it, while irrationalism must tend to discourage it. (Vol. ii, 239)

In the last section of the chapter Popper selected A. J. Toynbee as an example of a brilliant scholar who was capable of exemplary research in his chosen field but lapsed into irrationalism on topics beyond his area of special expertise.

Chapter 25: Has History Any Meaning

In this chapter Popper emerged as something of an existentialist (without hysteria) with the message that history has no meaning but we can give it meaning!

Section I explains the importance of theories and/or points of view to organize our selection of historical facts from the vast amount of information that is available. Section II is a more detailed account of the role of theories in scientific research. Section III explains the role of problems, issues or points of view in compiling historical narratives. Section IV focuses on the question of meaning and purpose in history.

Nearing the end of the book he described his effort as "merely scattered marginal notes" on a history of the error that he labelled historicism, "and rather personal notes to boot." He did not mean that everything in the book is a matter of opinion, rather he meant that he exercised more freedom to exercise personal choice than scientists normally enjoy. This difference is a matter of degree because even the data assembled in (natural) scientific research is not merely a 'body of facts', it is to some extent a collection that depends on the collector's interests, that is, on a point of view. This would appear to open the door for the subjectivism and the sociology of science but that is not really the case. Scientific investigation is guided by the theories that are "in play" at the time, by the need to test them, apply them, criticize them and improve them.

In historical studies the organizing principles are not general theories but problems, issues, and narratives, leading to multiple interpretations of history.

> But this does not mean, of course, that all interpretations are of equal merit. First, there are always interpretations which are not really in keeping with the accepted records; secondly, there are some which need a number of more or less plausible auxiliary hypotheses if they are to escape falsification by the records; next, there are some that are unable to connect a number of facts which another interpretation can connect, and in so far 'explain'. There may accordingly be a considerable amount of progress even within the field of historical interpretation. (Vol. ii, 266)

The proliferation of narratives and points of view is not an invitation to relativism because all interpretations have to stand up to criticism and historians need to be conscious of their own point of view, to be willing to reconsider it, and to avoid as much as possible giving in to unconscious bias in the selection and interpretation of facts. Of course the selection of evidence is just that, selective, but the point is to use the evidence in a critical and not an uncritical manner. As a public document the historical narrative will have to stand up to criticism from other people who may not be charitably inclined towards the views of the author. Desirable features of the story in addition to its capacity to stand up to criticism will include its fertility, its ability to prompt fresh ideas and elucidate new sources of information, also its topical interest and the way it illuminates the problems of the day.

The meaning of history

The question of destiny and our role in the great historical narrative brings us back to the starting point of the book, to Popper's criticism of the idea of historical determinism and the notion that there is a great plan that is being played out. Is there a meaning in history?

Popper answered "No!" because history has no meaning . To make his meaning clearer he wrote that "history" in the sense of a single "story" simply does not exist. There is an indefinite number of histories but the history of political power was given the special privilege of being the history of the world.

> But this, I hold, is an offence against every decent conception of mankind. It is hardly better than to treat the history of embezzlement or of robbery or of poisoning as the history of mankind. *For the history of power politics is nothing but the history of international crime and mass murder* (including, it is true, some of the attempts to suppress them). This history is taught in schools, and some of the greatest criminals are extolled as its heroes. (Vol. ii, 270)

This is a dangerous situation and it easily leads to the corruption of historians and to the propagation of uncritical, even worshipful, attitudes towards strong leaders, just because they were strong and successful, regardless of the harm they did. This thought led Popper into some extended commentary on the Christian view of history and the extent to which this has helped or hindered good historical research and writing. It also led him to some criticisms of Hegel by Kierkegaard and

Schopenhauer regarding the tone of historical writing especially among nationalistic German academics.

> And, indeed, our intellectual as well as our ethical education is corrupt. It is perverted by the admiration of brilliance, of the way things are said, which takes the place of a critical appreciation of the things that are said (and the things that are done). It is perverted by the romantic idea of the splendour of the stage of History on which we are the actors. We are educated to act with an eye to the gallery. (Vol. ii, 275)

The book ends with a flourish!

> History has no meaning, I contend. But this contention does not imply that all we can do about it is to look aghast at the history of political power, or that we must look on it as a cruel joke. For we can interpret it, with an eye to those problems of power politics whose solution we choose to attempt in our time. We can interpret the history of power politics from the point of view of our fight for the open society, for a rule of reason, for justice, freedom, equality, and for the control of international crime. Although history has no ends, we can impose these ends of ours upon it; and *although history has no meaning, we can give it a meaning.* (Vol. ii, 278)

CHAPTER FIVE

THE POVERTY OF HISTORICISM

Why *The Poverty of Historicism* matters

The Poverty of Historicism is a short book on the methods of the social sciences and social reform. It appeared as a series of three journal articles in 1944/45.

It refuted the major arguments which propped up the belief in "Inexorable Laws of Historical Development", one of the most dangerous and damaging myths of modern times. It is a neglected classic because it was overshadowed by *The Open Society and Its Enemies* which appeared in 1945 while *The Poverty of Historicism* did not appear in book form until 1957.

In the context of Popper's lifetime achievement it is the work where he first developed the ideas of institutional analysis and the logic of the situation. Allied with work by Talcott Parsons and Ludwig von Mises, these ideas could have changed the direction of developments in economics and the other social sciences after WWII.

Popper brought his work on the philosophy of physics to bear on the methods of the social sciences to transform them in the same way that he transformed the philosophy of the natural sciences in *Logik der Forschung* (1935). This had a moral and political purpose because he believed that defective methods in the social sciences contributed to the rise of fascism and communism. The book is dedicated to the victims of these movements.

In the Preface he spelled out a strictly logical argument to show that is impossible to predict the future course of history. The case can be summarized: (1) The course of human history is strongly influenced by the growth of human knowledge. (2) We cannot predict, by rational or scientific methods, the future growth of our scientific knowledge. (3) Therefore we cannot predict the future course of history.

He wanted the social sciences to develop a body of practical knowledge or social technology to deliver peace, freedom and prosperity in the way that industrial and agricultural technologies increased the productive capacity of the earth. This knowledge and the kind of social reforms that he advocated would be subject to abuse, like science and technology, but not nearly as much as grand schemes driven by dictators or "philosopher kings" who believe that "history is on our side".

A window of opportunity

The chapter Popper's Progress noted how Popper in the 1930s developed a program for the social sciences which is similar to that of the American Talcott Parsons and another Austrian, Ludwig von Mises. This opened a window of opportunity for an exchange of ideas and a united stand against some of the unhelpful methods that dominated the social sciences after World War II. However there was no united front and the three scholars hardly even referred to each other in print.

Two problems of reception

1. Popper's use of the term historicism.

2. The organization of the book.

Historicism

When Popper started to develop these ideas in the 1930s the term historicism was not in general use and he felt free to define it to suit his own purpose. However by 1957 it was circulating in English with several related but not identical connotations.

> I mean by 'historicism' an approach to the social sciences which

> assumes that *historical prediction* is the principal aim, and which
> assumes that this aim is attainable by discovering the 'rhythms' or
> the 'patterns', the 'laws' or the 'trends' of history. (3)

This could be called the "the locomotive theory of history", with the implication that people should submit to the power of revolutionary historical forces. At the time these forces appeared to be sweeping away democracy in favour of communism in the east and national socialism in Germany and Italy.

The plan of the book

Popper identified two sets of ideas which either propped up the doctrine of historical inevitability or in other ways undermined the efforts of people trying to put in place realistic programs of social improvement. One of these sets of ideas he called the anti-naturalistic doctrines of historicism because they opposed the use of the methods of the natural sciences in the human sciences. The other set he called the pro-naturalistic doctrines of historicism because they argued that there is a scientific case for historical determinism. Fresh from his revolutionary work in the philosophy of physics, Popper was convinced that both groups had misread the play in the natural sciences.

The book has four parts:

I. The anti-naturalistic doctrines of historicism.

II. The pro-naturalistic doctrines of historicism.

III. Criticism of the anti-naturalistic doctrines.

IV. Criticism of the pro-naturalistic doctrines.

The plan looks neat but the critical sections do not completely match the structure of the first two parts. Ian Jarvie's commentary is helpful (Jarvie, 1982). Possibly the fourth part was completed under pressure of time because some sections contain very brief statements of important ideas which called for more explanation and application. That especially applies to his analysis of scientific and industrial progress in institutional rather than psychological terms.

I: The anti-naturalistic doctrines of historicism

Part I contains ten sections, each devoted to a particular reason why the methods of physics cannot be used in the social sciences.

1. Generalisation.

2. Experiment.

3. Novelty.

4. Complexity.

5. Inexactitude of prediction.

6. Objectivity and valuation.

7. Holism.

8. Intuitive understanding.

9. Quantitative methods.

10. Essentialism versus nominalism.

To summarise these arguments: it is often claimed that the human sciences cannot find the kind of universal laws that Newton discovered in physics, due to the complexity of social systems and the novelties that arise in social evolution. Those complications also preclude the use of controlled experiments and give rise to insuperable problems in the precise measurement of variables and the accurate prediction of events.

Hopes, fears and political beliefs intrude, and so there is a need for "intuitive understanding" of the meaning of actions which does not arise in the case of events in the non-human world. For that reason there has to be much more attention to the nuances of language, and the "deeper" or "essential" meaning of terms. These ideas are subjected to criticism in part III.

II: The pro-naturalistic doctrines of historicism

This part introduces some of the beliefs which people held to support the quest for scientific laws of historical development. They were inspired by the success of Newton's theory in predicting celestial events long before they happened and they looked to historical studies to deliver the "laws of motion" of social and economic systems.

11. Comparison with astronomy, long-term forecasts and large-scale forecasts.

12. The observational basis.

13. Social dynamics.

14. Historical laws.

15. Historical prophecy vs social engineering.

16. The theory of historical development.

17. Interpreting vs planning social change.

18. Conclusion of the analysis.

The pro-naturalists drew on the immense authority of Newton and Darwin among progressive thinkers in the nineteenth century. They were especially impressed with the apparent capacity of physics to explain practically every mechanical event under the sun and especially to provide long-term predictions of the movements and location of celestial bodies.

Parallel with this was an obsession with history and historical change among discontents who yearned for radical reforms. Many were inspired by the belief that Marx had laid bare the economic laws of motion of human society.

Due to the problems of complexity and measurement the pro-naturalists were prepared to give up the possibility of predicting events in fine detail and instead they aimed for broad, large-scale forecasts. Historical studies, rather than the observations and experiments of the scientists, would provide the empirical base of the new social sciences. For the historicists, sociology is theoretical history and economics is a branch of historical studies.

The "iron laws of history" would be the drivers of social change. These are not the same as the universal and unchanging laws that were sought by the classical economists in the manner of natural scientists. For the historicist the laws of society must be the laws which link up the successive periods. They are *laws of historical development*.

As for planning social change, Marx famously heaped scorn on reformers who wanted to undertake deliberate changes to steadily improve social conditions. He dismissed them as utopians. For historicists following Marx, the purpose of theoretical history was to identify forthcoming changes (hopefully revolutionary changes) and adjust to them, or perhaps help them along. Deliberately planning reforms in consultation with the people involved and then checking the results in a "laboratory scientific" manner was out of the question.

III: Criticism of the anti-naturalistic doctrines

The third and fourth parts of the book contain Popper's rejoinder to both kinds of historicists and also his positive views, especially in sections 19 to 21 in part III and sections 28 to 32 in Part IV.

19. Practical aims of this criticism.

20. The technological approach to sociology.

21. Piecemeal versus utopian engineering.

22. The unholy alliance with utopianism.

23. Criticism of holism.

24. The holistic theory of social experiments.

25. The variability of experimental conditions.

26. Are generalizations confined to periods.

On the practical aims of the criticism, Popper did not really care whether scientific investigators are motivated by practical concerns or the search for truth because both objectives can be pursued at the same time by a good selection of problems and also by effective communication between pure and applied researchers. As for debates on methods, he wrote that fruitful methodological debates usually arise out of practical problems which confront working scientists "...and nearly all debates that are not so inspired are characterized by that atmosphere of futile subtlety which has brought methodology into disrepute with the practical research worker" (57).

He was prepared to take a stand with historicists on the common ground of concern for better methods to transform the social sciences to make them more helpful for public administrators, politicians and would-be social reformers.

The technological approach (section 20)

> The term social technology is likely to arouse suspicion, and to repel those whom it reminds of the social blueprints of the collectivist planners, or perhaps even of the technocrats. I realise this danger, and so I have added the word 'piecemeal', both to offset undesirable associations and to express my conviction that 'piecemeal tinkering' (as it is sometimes called) combined with critical analysis, is the main way to practical results in the social as well as in the natural sciences. (58)

Popper's attempt to anticipate criticism did not succeed. Hayek was not happy with Popper's terminology because he was obsessed with the danger of large-scale central planning. Ludwig von Mises attacked social engineering in scathing terms without ever mentioning that the kind of social engineering that Popper preached was the kind of activity which von Mises himself practiced every day when he was an advisor to the Austrian government.

Mises argued that government interventions in the marketplace almost inevitably fail to produce the desired effects. He was in favour of better government policy because he was not a zero state anarchist, and he should have realised that the Popperian approach is neutral as to whether a particular problem calls for more government action, or less (deregulation) or none at all.

Practical people who work with machinery usually check very carefully to see if their tinkering (intervention) makes the thing work better or not. That is the mentality that Popper thought should be applied to social institutions. He advocated this approach to all social problems and policy issues, whether private or public. Examples of private issues are the administration and organization of private firms and the productivity of the workforce. Public issues which Popper nominated include tax policy, the state budget, controlling the trade cycle, the feasibility of central planning and one that is very relevant at the present time, the question of how to export democracy to the Middle East.

The focus on practical problems does not preclude an interest in theoretical problems but it does control the tendency for theory to degenerate into speculative metaphysics especially under the influence of extended conceptual analysis, that is, the error of "essentialism" as Popper called it.

Piecemeal vs utopian engineering (section 21)

> Just as the main task of the physical engineer is to design machines and to remodel and service them, the task of the piecemeal social engineer is to design social institutions, and to reconstruct and run those already in existence" (64)

Popper articulated the Scottish/Austrian doctrine that only a minority of social institutions are consciously designed, and most have grown as the unintended consequences of human actions. The piecemeal reformer will proceed in stages, alert to the results of his tinkering (so far as these can be assessed), like a mechanic building a machine or tuning an engine. In contrast the utopian engineer is inclined to be in a hurry to realise grand schemes. These may involve the remodelling of the whole of society, more or less regardless of the results.

Pressed for an answer to the question "What is the difference between piecemeal and radical engineering?" Popper did not draw a precise line of demarcation between the two methods. It is more illuminating to focus on the mindset of the reformer and the way that major reforms are attempted. The holist (whole-system) planner considers that the piecemeal approach is incapable of producing the sweeping reforms that are required to sweep out the old and bring in the brand new. But Popper pointed out that when the revolutionaries are in charge they find they are forced to make piecemeal changes, albeit large and sweeping, in a haphazard, clumsy and often brutal manner. "Thus the difference turns out in practice to be a difference not so much in scale and scope as in caution and in preparedness for unavoidable surprises." (69).

The remaining sections in this part address various ideas which impede the critical evaluation of social reforms and especially state interventions. Interventions call for careful evaluation in terms of clearly stated objectives and outcome indicators (measures of performance). If this control is not in place then the temptation is overwhelming for the planners to persist with failing programs or even to demand more of the same rather than admit that the initial reform was a mistake.

The unholy alliance with utopianism (sections 22, 23 & 24)

Popper noted that the kind of leaders who want to press ahead with grand schemes tend to have advisors who tell them what they want to hear, so it is practically impossible to impose the rigors of criticism and testing on the Utopian experiment. The result of this is now history in places like Russia, China and Cambodia. On a lesser level of damage, similar principles apply in the Big Government bureaucracies of the modern democracies especially in response to perceived crises of national security (the war or terror") or the drug problem (the war on drugs).

The criticism of holism in section 23 can be formulated as a critique of inappropriate or misleading aggregation (grouping of data) which has become a major issue since the rise of Keynesian demand management.

In section 24 on the holistic theory of social experiments Popper raised the power and information problem.

> The holistic planner overlooks the fact that it is easy to centralize power but impossible to centralize all the knowledge which is distributed over many individual minds. Unable to ascertain what is in the minds of so many individuals, he must try to simplify his problems by eliminating individual differences by education and propaganda. (90)

Experiments, complexity & social laws (sections 25 & 26)

Historicists think that the complexity of social systems eliminates the experimental approach. Popper insisted that the problems of variety, complexity and change arise in the natural sciences, especially biology and geology, and they can be met by appropriate methods of investigation and analysis. The claim that there cannot be experimental studies in economics (articulated by Ludwig von Mises) is now confronted by a thriving industry of experimental economics.

On the topic of complexity Popper suggested that the problem in the social sciences is inflated because real physical systems are also complicated and that is usually regarded as a challenge and not an overwhelming problem. He even suggested that the human capacity for planning and purposeful action could be used to simplify the analysis of social systems by way of a "rationality principle".

> Admittedly, human beings hardly ever act quite rationally [as they would if they made the best use of all the available information on the situation] but they act more or less rationally; and this makes it

possible to construct comparatively simple models of their actions and inter-actions, and to use these models as approximations. (140-41)

He advocated the search for laws in economics and sociology and he suggested some examples; "You cannot introduce agricultural tariffs and at the same time reduce the cost of living", "You cannot have a centrally planned society with a price system that fulfils the main function of competitive prices", "You cannot have full employment without inflation" (62).

However for historical studies the approach using explanatory laws is less helpful than the approach using the rationality principle, and he turned to another approach which he called the "zero method", borrowed from neoclassical economics.

By this I mean the method of constructing a model on the assumption of complete rationality (and perhaps also on the assumption of the possession of complete information) on the part of all the individuals concerned, and of estimating the deviation of the actual behaviour of people from the model behaviour, using the latter as a kind of zero coordinate. (141)

Later this approach evolved into the method of Situational Analysis and the Rationality Principle which does not assume perfect knowledge and insight but works with the actual plans and intentions of actors, so far as they can be worked out using the available evidence.

IV: Criticism of the pro-naturalistic doctrines of historicism

This part covers many issues and concludes with a highly condensed treatment of one of the most important ideas in the book, namely the need for institutional and situational analysis in the social sciences, especially to understand scientific and industrial progress. This part of the book appears to be a rushed job, with some problems of organization. For example section 31 contains material that would have been better placed in the preceding section.

27. Is there a law of evolution? Laws and trends.

28. The method of reduction. Causal explanation, prediction and prophecy.

29. The unity of method.

30. Theoretical and historical sciences.

31. Situational logic in history. Historical interpretation.

32. The institutional theory of progress.

33. Conclusion.

Laws and trends (section 27)

The success of long-term predictions in astronomy inspired Marx and Marxists when they spoke of discovering the laws of motion of the social system. However long-term predictions in astronomy depend on the stability and relative isolation of the solar system and that kind of stability is precisely what is denied by people who are interested in major historical changes, like revolutions.

Popper explained that the attempt to recruit the methods of science to predict the future course of history did not take account of the difference between laws and trends, and between prediction and prophecy. Valid laws of the IF -> THEN kind can be used, along with a statement of the initial conditions, to deduce a prediction (IF an apple is dropped in a gravitational field, THEN it will fall). However this does not mean that a trend will persist unless the conditions remain the same (the apple stops falling when it reaches the ground).

The method of reduction, causal explanation, prediction and prophecy (section 28)

In this section Popper restated the deductive model of explanation that he spelled out in *Logik der Forschung*. This achieved wide fame when Hempel and Oppenheim published a paper in English on the nomological-deductive or "covering law" model of explanation. In this model, a combination of general laws and initial conditions (which represent the cause) permits the deduction of an event (the effect).

The prediction also stands as an explanation. So a general law (of gravity) plus a situation (an unrestrained apple) explains the effect (the apple falls).

On explanation, prediction and testing

> The use of a theory for predicting is just another aspect of its use for explaining such an event. And since we test a theory by comparing the events predicted with those actually observed, our analysis also shows how theories can be tested. Whether we use a theory for the purpose of explanation, or prediction, or of testing, depends upon our interest; it depends upon the question which statements we consider as given or unproblematic, and which statements we consider to stand in need of further criticism, and of testing. (123)

So a physicist can test the law of gravity by setting up a situation with an unconstrained apple to see what happens. A historian who is interested in the fall of a particular apple at a particular time will assume that the law of gravity is unproblematic and will focus on the situation to explain the event. Did the apple fall or was it pushed?

In section 29 on the unity of method Popper argued that all generalizing sciences use the same deductive model of explanation.

In section 30 on the theoretical and historical sciences Popper expanded on the point that was made briefly above regarding the falling apple. The same model of explanation applies in each but in history the focus of interest is not the general theories but the particular events, that is, the situation and what happened ("Who pushed the apple?").

Historical interpretation

Popper explained the different organising principles for theoretical and historical studies. In theoretical studies (conducted by the generalizing sciences), work is organised around the comparison and testing of *general explanatory theories*. These theories are used to explain specific events and sometimes for technological purposes (though not as much as we tend to assume), for example designing structures in mechanical engineering and policies and institutions in social engineering.

Work in historical studies is organized around points of view, issues of interest and narratives. There are many narratives and the test of truth (as well as other criteria like relevance and consistency) can be applied. Popper noted that the historicists got into trouble by elevating points of view to the status of universal explanatory theories, and so the class struggle was applied to history to explain everything. This can be illuminating but it can also be overdone because the class struggle does not explain everything.

That broad-brush approach aroused a reaction from the people who Talcott Parsons called the "particularists" or "objectivists" who thought that objectivity means refraining from selecting facts under the influence of a point of view. They thought that *the truth should emerge from the accumulation of particular pieces of information* (there is a clear parallel with the form of empiricism which is supposed to start with collections of facts). Of course there is no way to avoid a point of view, or at least a purpose for the historical study, and it is essential to be clear about the point of view (or the purpose), to state it plainly and point out that it is one among many.

Situational logic in history (section 31)

This section could have been split in two, the first continuing the theme of historical interpretation from the previous section and the second taking up the very important idea of situational logic or situational analysis.

Alan Donagan wrote in the Schilpp volume on Popper that Popper's critique of historicism had positive as well as negative (critical) aspects. The major positives are the theory of situational logic in history, and the institutional theory of progress. (Donegan, 1974, 923).

This section gives a preliminary sketch of the situational logic or situational analysis which became one of Popper's signature ideas. It is an extremely compact statement about the need for institutional studies.

> Beyond this logic of situations, or perhaps as a part of it, we need something like an analysis of social movements. We need studies, based on methodological individualism, of the social institutions through which ideas may spread and captivate individuals, of the way in which new traditions may be created, and of the way in which traditions work and break down. (149)

This can be seen as a call for the kind of work that Douglas North pursued to win a Nobel Prize in Economics in 1993. In his acceptance speech he stated "Institutions form the incentive structure of a society and the political and economic institutions, in consequence, are the underlying determinant of economic performance." Economic Performance Through Time, December 1993.
http://www.nobelprize.org/nobel_prizes/economic-sciences/laureates/1993/north-lecture.html

That is the point which Popper made briefly in the following section.

The institutional theory (section 32)

Popper advocated institutional analysis as an alternative to the psychological approach of Comte and Mill to explain the phenomenon of human progress. They believed that progress in science and industry is an absolute trend, based on the progressive tendency of the human mind. Popper noted that there are other tendencies of the human mind like forgetfulness, indolence and dogmatism.

> This immediately leads to the realization that a psychological propensity alone cannot be sufficient to explain progress, since conditions may be found on which it may depend. Thus we must, next, replace the theory of psychological propensities by something better; I suggest, by an *institutional* (and technological) analysis of the conditions of progress. (154)

136

He suggested that a more tenable theory will address the *conditions* of progress, and he addressed this in a rather counter-intuitive way by trying to imagine conditions under which progress would be *arrested*. For example he suggested that might be achieved by closing down (or subjecting to political control) laboratories for research, scientific periodicals, congresses and conferences, universities and printing presses. This is a part of his take on the social nature of science, spelled out in Chapter 23 of *The Open Society* (an early sign of the "social turn" described by Ian Jarvie).

> Science, and more especially scientific progress, are the results not of isolated efforts but of the free competition of thought. For science needs ever more competition between hypotheses and ever more rigorous tests. And the competing hypotheses need personal representation, as it were: they need advocates, they need a jury, and even a public. This personal representation must be institutionally organized if we wish to ensure that it works. And these institutions have to be paid for, and protected by law. Ultimately, progress depends very largely on political factors; on political institutions that safeguard the freedom of thought: on democracy. (155)

Conclusion

Popper concluded the book with some speculation about the emotional appeal of laws of historical development. He described this as a very ancient idea, originally mythological in nature and drawing on biological models such as the life cycles of plants, or to theological ideas about the chosen people. The modern versions draw more obviously from science but are not more credible or helpful for that reason.

CHAPTER SIX

CONJECTURES AND REFUTATIONS

CONTENTS

Introduction

As we learn from our mistakes our knowledge grows, even though we may never know - that is, know for certain. Since our knowledge can grow, there can be no scope here for despair of reason. And since we can never know for certain, there can be no authority here for any claim to authority, for conceit over our knowledge, or for smugness. (Preface)

Why *Conjectures and Refutations* matters

The papers in this 1963 collection brought the full range and depth of Popper's work to the attention of the educated public. After *The Open Society and Its Enemies* in 1945 there was little outside the academic journals to indicate the amount of ground that Popper covered until *The Poverty of Historicism* appeared in 1957, followed by *The Logic of Scientific Discovery* in 1959. However neither of those volumes indicated the diversity of Popper's interests or provided an accessible introduction to his thought.

During the 1950s his range of influence was almost entirely limited to the undergraduate students at the London School of Economics who attended his annual series of lectures on the philosophy of science and also the people who attended his regular Tuesday seminar.

The 21 papers in this collection include an important fragment of intellectual biography. Some of the best papers in this collection deserve the status of classics, such as the Introduction, "On the sources of knowledge and of ignorance", which challenged the authoritarian structure of western thought and inspired Bartley's program to unpack the implications of "non-justificationism".

Chapter 1 contains some autobiographical notes and it reveals how Popper's psychological studies on habit-formation paid off by adding value to his ideas on epistemology. An appendix contains a long list of his research projects in the 1950s.

Chapter 2 is a seminal paper on the way extra-philosophical problems vitalize and enrich philosophical investigations. He warned that philosophy could become introverted and marginalized if those external "roots" are cut. It seems that the philosophers were not paying attention because Mulligan, Simon and Smith sounded the same warning several decades later (Mulligan et al 2006).

Chapter 3 demarcated his theory of conjectural knowledge from the rival schools of essentialism and instrumentalism. Chapter 4, "Towards a rational theory of tradition", sought a middle way between rigid traditionalism and the stance of the "adversary culture" which treats all traditions with contempt.

Chapter 5 is a tribute to the philosophers before Socrates who invented the tradition of criticism which animated the progress of western science and civilization. Chapter 8 represents a major break with the anti-metaphysical stance of most of the philosophers of science at the time. Chapter 12 gives a glimpse of the approach to language that he took from Karl Buhler and later elaborated in connection with his ideas on evolution and objective knowledge.

Chapter 17 is a statement of classical liberal principles including the role of the "moral framework" and the vital importance of free speech and critical public discussion. Chapter 18 is a critique of the idea of "self-determinism" for national, ethnic or racial collectives, surely one of the most dangerous ideas since historicism and fascism.

Timing matters: the tyranny of fads and fashions

As noted in the chapter Popper's Progress, during the 1950s various forms of linguistic philosophy became popular among analytical philosophers and in 1961 Kuhn appeared on the scene. Consequently Popper's work was published against the tide of philosophical thinking. Without the excitement and distraction caused by *The Structure of Scientific Revolutions*, the publication of *Conjectures and Refutations* could have been seen as an exciting development with important contributions to many issues and making ground-breaking progress with some of them.

Introduction: On the Sources of Knowledge and of Ignorance

Popper delivered this long paper to the British Academy in 1960. He identified the authoritarian structure of western epistemology and political philosophy, based on the quest for "justified true beliefs" which are certified by the appropriate authority. The first half of the paper notes the historical roots of the two major schools of thought, the Continental or Rationalist tradition that the truth derives from "clear and distinct ideas" and the Empiricist tradition that sense experience is the authority. Both promote the idea that the truth is manifest to those who are willing to grasp it.

Popper traced a link between that optimistic epistemology of "manifest truth" and the modern movements of political liberalism. He also noted the downside of that optimism about the truth in the form of the "conspiracy theory of ignorance".

The paper charts the historical roots of optimistic and pessimistic epistemologies from Homer and Hesiod to Plato, then to Bacon and Descartes with some space devoted to the quest the true meaning of terms (essentialism) and an introduction to the "Table of Opposites" which Popper used to clarify his position on the function of definitions.

In the second half of the paper Popper presented a solution to the dilemma of rival authorities . He suggested that there are no authorities and the quest for the true source of beliefs is unfounded because there are many sources of ideas but none can be regarded as the authority.

Epistemology and political liberalism

> The great movement of liberation that started in the Renaissance and led through the many vicissitudes of the reformation and the religious and revolutionary wars to the free societies in which the English-speaking people are privileged to live, this movement was inspired throughout by an unparalleled epistemological optimism: by a most optimistic view of man's power to discern truth and to acquire knowledge. (5)

Popper noted that even an abstract study like epistemology can be motivated, perhaps unconsciously, by political hopes and dreams. He suggested that this should be a warning to us. But what can we do about it? He confessed to being a liberal, in the English, non-collectivist sense. "But just because I am a liberal I feel that few things are more important for a liberal than to submit the various theories of liberalism to a searching critical examination" (6). He found that many of the ideas and doctrines which had inspired political liberals are not tenable, including the doctrine of the manifest truth and the inevitability of progress.

The conspiracy theory of ignorance

As Popper explored the ideas that underpinned liberalism, he encountered what he called the conspiracy theory of ignorance. This is based on a line of thought that runs - *if the truth is clear to honest and clear-eyed seekers, then if they fall into error, or promulgate it, either their motivation is suspect or they have been taken in and deluded or led astray by some other evil person or group.*

In his opinion that false epistemology was the major inspiration for an intellectual and moral revolution "without parallel in history". It encouraged independent thought and the rational Enlightenment belief that knowledge could set people free from servitude and misery.

> It made modern science possible. It became the basis of the fight against censorship and the suppression of free thought...It made men feel responsible for themselves and for others, and eager to improve not only their own condition but also that of their fellow men. (8)

Unfortunately there was a downside because many good ideas were inspired by a bad one, notably the theory that truth is manifest. Popper argued that this false epistemology led to disastrous consequences because it became the basis of almost every kind of fanaticism. "For only the most depraved wickedness can refuse to see the manifest truth; only those who have reason to fear truth conspire to suppress it." (8)

Solving the problem: a critique of empiricism

This section of the lecture is a critique of empiricism, that is, the doctrine that knowledge has to rest on the firm foundations of observations in the form of sense impressions or memories based on evidence obtained by way of the senses. Popper suggested that the program of asking for observational sources violates commonsense because the normal procedure to handle uncertainty about a report of an event, for example in a newspaper, is to look for another report.

The authoritarian structure of traditional philosophy

The traditional systems of epistemology are dominated by yes-answers and no-answers to questions about the sources or authorities for our knowledge. Popper noted the authoritarian spirit in those questions and he drew a comparison with the traditional question of political theory,

"Who should rule?" which begs for an authoritarian answer such as "the best", or "the people", or "the majority". He suggested that the question is wrongly put and he explained in chapter 7 of *The Open Society* that the answers are paradoxical. He proposed that in politics the authoritarian question should be replaced by a completely different one, such as "How can we organise our political institutions so that bad or incompetent rulers cannot do too much damage?" (25).

Questions about the authoritative sources of our knowledge can be replaced in a similar way by paying attention to the various forms of criticism that can be used to test ideas:

1.   The check on problem-solving capacity of the theory or the policy.

2.   Internal consistency.

3.   Consistency with other well-tested theories or policies.

4.   The test of evidence.

5.   The test of metaphysics, consistency with the metaphysical research program.

William W. Bartley was a very interested listener in the audience when Popper delivered this lecture and he was inspired to purse his ambitious program on the implications of Popper's "non-justificationist" approach for the theory and the "ecology" of rationality. This provided an explanation of Popper's struggle to get traction in the profession because the theory of conjectural knowledge does not sit comfortably alongside the programs which are concerned with verification, justification and confirmation.

Chapter 1: Science - Conjectures and Refutations

This lecture was a contribution to a series of talks on developments and trends in British philosophy. Delivered in 1953, it appeared as "Philosophy of Science: A Personal Report" in *British Philosophy in Mid-Century* (ed. C. A. Mace, 1957).

144

This is Popper's first piece of intellectual autobiography, with an account of his early suspicions about the scientific status of psychoanalysis and Marxism in the form that they were expounded by dogmatic followers. Einstein's very different attitude towards testing prompted the idea of the falsifiability criterion for science, in contrast with the verificationist approach of the positivists.

> My attacks upon verification soon led to complete confusion in the camp of the verificationist philosophers of sense and nonsense. The original proposal of verifiability as the criterion of meaning was at least clear, simple, and forceful. The modifications and shifts which were now introduced were the very opposite. (41)

He explained how his work on demarcation and his criticism of Wittgenstein's views on verification led in two directions, (1) to reject the obsession with "meaning" and (2) to see a solution to the problem of induction as it was posed by Hume.

His response to Hume was informed by his thoughts on demarcation and also by his 1927 doctoral research on habit formation in children. This turned out to have unexpected relevance to the problem of induction. He also mentioned another interest which contributed. "In fact my ideas about induction originated in a conjecture about the evolution of Western polyphony. But you will be spared this story." (50).

He concluded that Hume's critique of the logic of inductive inference was valid but his psychological explanation of habit formation and our belief in the regularities of the world (based on repetition of experiences) was not. Logical considerations moved him to replace the psychological theory of induction with the Kantian idea that we actively attempt to impose regularities on the world. We jump to conclusions, though our conclusions may not be correct. "These may have to be discarded later, should observations show they are wrong" (46). This was the genesis of his theory of conjecture and refutations, of learning by trial and error.

In section VIII of the paper he turned from the psychology of experience to his central concern, the logic of science. "It was easy to see that the method of science is criticism, i.e. attempted falsification. Yet it took me a few years to notice that the two problems - of demarcation and of induction - were in a sense one." (52).

Hume was concerned with the **problem of justification**, that is, the justification of beliefs in regularities in nature on the basis of observations. But if we accept fallibilism and conjectural knowledge (meaning that our beliefs can be wrong) **the quest for justification is replaced by testing** (attempted falsification) and Hume's problem ceases to be "the skeleton in the cupboard of scientific rationality".

Popper's research program in 1953

The frequency theory of probability.

The propensity interpretation of probability.

The use of statistics to test probability statements.

A number of problems with the formalism of quantum theory.

The problem of determinism.

The problem of simplicity in scientific theories.

Degrees of 'ad hocness' in scientific theories.

The relation between layers of explanatory hypotheses in highly developed theoretical sciences.

Problems raised by instrumentalism and operationalism, including the need for a general theory of measurement to take account of the theory-dependence of observations.

The problem of explanation, including degrees of explanatory power and the relationship between explanation and prediction.

Explanation in history and the social sciences.

The nature of scientific objectivity in relation to the sociology of science.

Responding to new approaches to induction.

Chapter 2: The Nature of Philosophical Problems and their Roots in Science

"We must beware of mistaking the well-nigh senseless and pointless subtleties of the imitators for the pressing and genuine problems of the pioneer." (96).

This chapter is based on a 1952 paper which Popper delivered to a meeting of the Philosophy of Science Group of the British Society for the History of Science.

He commenced by stating that he was not happy to talk about the present position of English philosophy because he thought it was more important to solve scientific or philosophical problems than to talk about what he or other philosophers are doing. Some years later it has turned out that this might have been a mistake because critical rationalism has been marginalised in the philosophy schools and it is possible that more attention to the state of play in the profession at large might have helped Popper and others who appreciated his ideas to compete more effectively for an audience.

On the description and classification of subjects

> Disciplines are distinguished partly for historical reasons and reasons of administrative convenience...But all this classification and distinction is a comparatively unimportant and superficial affair. *We are not students of some subject matter but students of problems.* And problems may cut right across the borders of any subject matter or discipline. (67)

Two theses

> Thesis 1. Every philosophy and every philosophical school is likely to degenerate under the influence of philosophical inbreeding to

the point where its problems become practically indistinguishable from pseudo-problems and its talk becomes almost meaningless babble. (71)

Popper's concern about the degeneration of philosophical schools in this paper of the 1950s was repeated by Mulligan, Simon and Smith in 2006 with a paper titled. "What's wrong with contemporary philosophy?" They noted that too many philosophers, in both the analytical and Continental traditions, are concerned with "in-house" puzzles and controversies that do not connect with live issues in science, politics and the world at large.

Thesis 2. The process of degeneration can be accelerated by the "prima facie" method of teaching philosophy, that is, starting off by reading the works of the great philosophers without reference to the problems outside philosophy which concerned them.

He pursued his case with two examples, the first is Plato's theory of Forms as a response to a crisis in number theory and the second example is Kant's *Critique of Pure Reason*.

The geometric program and the Theory of Forms

Popper depicted the Theory of Forms as a response to the problem in number theory that arose with the discovery of the irrational numbers. These are numbers that cannot be written as a simple fraction or a simple ratio of whole numbers. Expressed as a decimal, the decimal goes on without reaching an end. Examples are the square roots of two and three. It is quite likely that this is the root of Popper's theory of research programs because he told the story in terms of the breakdown of the Pythagorean program to reduce geometry and cosmology to arithmetic and out of that failure came the rise of a new geometrical cosmology.

The argument can be summarised in a number of points:

1.   Pythagorianism and atomism were based on arithmetic (counting).

2.	Plato recognized the catastrophic implications of the discovery of the irrational numbers.

3.	The sign over the gates of Plato's Academy read "Nobody untrained in geometry may enter my house". Geometry was the science of the incommensurables or irrationals, in contrast with arithmetic which treats "the odds and evens" (integers and their relations).

4.	Euclid's *Elements* can be seen as a summary of the attempt in the Platonic school to reconstruct epistemology and cosmology on the basis of geometry.

5.	Plato contributed to the program, especially in developing solid geometry.

6.	In the *Timaeus* Plato spelled out a geometrical version of atomic theory to construct the famous "Platonic bodies" using triangles incorporating the (irrational) square roots of two and three.

7.	Plato advanced the idea of making geometrical models of the world, especially models to describe the movements of the planets.

In Popper's opinion Euclid's geometry was not just a textbook of pure geometry but an attempt to provide theory of the world (a cosmology). In his lectures Popper taught that Euclid was not properly understood in modern times because he neglected to state explicitly that (1) the Platonic school was doing cosmology and (2) his book was a summary of solutions without any mention of the unsolved problems. He did not need to say it because everyone at the time knew about the problems in the background but the historical context was forgotten over the centuries as Euclid's *Principles* became the standard textbook of geometry. Eventually the test of a certified "geometer" became knowing the principles, not the capacity to identify problems and advance the subject.

Popper pursued the story in considerable depth to explain how Plato combined his work on geometry, cosmology and epistemology;

including the idea of explaining the visible by postulating an invisible world of causes.

Kant's *Critique of Pure Reason*

Popper had great respect for Kant and he spelled out the problem situation that Kant confronted to explain why he admired Kant so much, even though Kant failed to provide a satisfactory solution to his problems.

> His *Critique of Pure Reason* is one of the most difficult books ever written. Kant wrote in great haste, and about a problem which, I shall try to show, was not only insoluble but also misconceived. Nevertheless it was not a pseudoproblem, but an inescapable problem which arose out of the contemporary situation of physical theory. (93)

Kant wrote for people who appreciated Newton's dynamics and the work of the great scientists Copernicus, Tycho Brahe, Kepler and Galileo who preceded him. Popper considered that the intellectuals of our own time are "spoilt and complacent" due to the triumphs of modern science and they do not fully understand the impact of Newton's theory. There were long periods of decay and recovery from the time when the ancient Presocratics daringly tackled the riddle of the Universe to the "staggering success" of Newton.

By the time Kant was at work no qualified commentator doubted that Newton's theory was true. It was a geometrical theory, modelled after Euclid, and it represented the gold which was always expected to be located at the end of the scientific quest.

> It had been tested by the most precise measurements, and it had always been right... An age-old dream had come true. Mankind had obtained knowledge, real, certain, indubitable, and demonstrable knowledge. (93)

Like everyone else, Kant accepted that Newton's theory was true but Hume roused him from what he called his "dogmatic slumber" with a logical analysis that wrecked the "inductive" foundations of science.

Thus Kant had to confront the dilemma that a true theory had apparently been discovered using a logically invalid process.

His response to this problem was his "Copernican Revolution" of the problem of knowledge. He proposed that knowledge was possible because our intellect makes up the laws and imposes them on nature. We do not passively receive sense data and discover the laws; in the language of Abrams book on literary theory, *The Mirror and the Lamp* the human mind functions as a lamp, not a mirror!

Popper considered Kant's theory to be a strange mixture of absurdity and truth, and Einstein provided the clue to a more satisfactory resolution when he demonstrated that even the best theory can be false.

The solution to Kant's dilemma was to reject Kant's assumption that Newton provided the final truth, and to accept a part of Kant's solution, that *we are the source of our theories*. We do not absorb information, we actively seek solutions, especially regularities in nature, we make up stories, we invent myths and we invent scientific theories. Then we subject them to criticism, including observational tests.

The point of Popper's two case studies was to demonstrate how some great philosophers found their problems and their inspiration from sources outside philosophy. The lesson is that modern philosophers need to keep in touch with the frontiers of knowledge in other fields. Agassi extended the ideas in this paper with "The Nature of Scientific Problems and Their Roots in Metaphysics" (Agassi, 1964).

Chapter 3: Three Views Concerning Human Knowledge

Popper's "third view" of scientific theories is that they are conjectures, "highly informative guesses about the world". They cannot be shown to be true but they can be severely tested. They can be very useful as instruments but at the same time they can (and should) be serious attempts to discover the truth.

This paper was written in 1956 as a part of his critique of instrumentalism in the philosophy of physics, especially in the Copenhagen interpretation of quantum theory. Similar arguments apply in other contexts such as the debate in the methods of economics that Milton Friedman triggered with his famous claim that prediction is all-important, regardless of the truth or realism of assumptions used for the predictions (Friedman, 1953).

The issue at stake in the modern debate is the way that instrumentalism has been adopted among physicists by default, without adequate critical discussion, under the influence of developments in quantum physics and especially the Copenhagen interpretation.

The chapter has six sections. The first describes the dispute between Galileo and Cardinal Bellarmino before the Inquisition. In the second section Popper spelled out the critical issue between Galileo and the church - whether the new science of celestial mechanics was true (or nearer to the truth than the pre-Copernican system) or whether it was merely a simpler and a more convenient instrument for astronomical calculations and predictions. The Church did not want science to become a competitor in the field of providing true statements about the cosmos although it had no problem with the invention of better instruments for navigation. Bishop Berkeley took the same line in his criticism of Newton's theory because, like Bellarmino before him, he wanted scientific theories to be regarded as convenient instruments for calculation and not as true descriptions of the world and the cosmos.

The third section of the paper is a critique of essentialism, the fourth section is a more detailed exposition of instrumentalism and the fifth section is a critique of that view. The sixth section is The Third View: Conjectures, Truth, and Reality.

The first view: ultimate explanation by essences

According to this view:

1.   The scientist aims to find a true theory or description of the world.

2.   The scientist can establish the truth of such theories.

3.   The best scientific theories describe the 'essential natures of things', the realities which lie behind the appearances.

The first proposition is part of the view that Popper defended. He contested 2 and 3.

Popper famously dissented from (2) in favour of the theory of conjectural knowledge, bearing in mind that the theories of concern are deep explanations using universal laws, not the existence of such things as particles or tables and chairs, and events such as the evolution of life on earth.

As to (3) Popper was not especially concerned to dispute the existence of "essences" that underlie the visible appearance of nature (he later called these "propensities). However he argued that the "essences" as they were understood at the moment were not the end of the road and the essentialist doctrine tends to stifle criticism and the search for deeper explanations beyond the current orthodoxy.

The second view: theories as instruments

This section includes a comparison of the three views and some exploration of the instrumentalist view, including some considerations of language and meaning which show that Popper could have excelled in language analysis if he ever thought that this was a worthwhile occupation.

Popper did not accept the instrumentalist view and he summed up his criticism as follows: Instrumentalism is the thesis that scientific theories are merely rules for calculation (or inference rules) like the computation rules of the applied sciences. In effect, there is no pure science and all science is applied.

> Now my reply to instrumentalism consists in showing that there are profound differences between pure theories and technological computation rules, and that instrumentalism can give a perfect

description of these rules but is quite unable to account for the difference between them and the theories. (p. 111)

The third view, conjectures, truth and reality

Popper suggested that instrumentalism is an ad hoc response to some serious problems with the interpretation of quantum theory, and it has the effect of deflecting criticism and limiting the field of search (or even the perceived need) for improved theories which meet the computational requirements and also provide a grip on the nature of reality.

Chapter 4: Towards a Rational Theory of Tradition

This was a talk delivered at the annual conference of the Rationalist Press Association on 26 July 1948, and published in *The Rationalist Annual* in 1949.

Popper took a "progressive" or critical reformist position, that is, the kind of position which secular humanists and rationalists usually to occupy. He mentioned some "anti-rationalist" arguments advanced by Michael Oakeshott in *Rationalism in Politics and Other Essays*. Surprisingly, an exchange of letters between Popper and Oakeshott showed that they were on the same side of the main issues. http://www.michael-oakeshott-association.com/pdfs/mo_letters_popper.pdf. This demonstrated the need to understand the very different interpretations that are attached to "rationalism" and rationality", to check which particular kind of rationality is under discussion and to appreciate the nuances that thinkers like Popper, Oakeshott and Hayek brought to bear on the topic.

Popper issued a warning to those humanists and rationalists who adopt a dismissive and contemptuous attitude towards traditions, saying "I am not interested in tradition, I want to judge everything on its own merits, independent of any tradition". Like Oakeshott and also Hayek, Popper saw the important role of traditions and the need to conserve valuable traditions while we criticise those that we see as dangerous or unhelpful.

> It should be clearly understood that there are only two main attitudes possible towards tradition. One is to accept a tradition uncritically, often without even being aware of it...The other possibility is a critical attitude, which may result either in acceptance or in rejection, or perhaps in a compromise. Yet we have to know of and to understand a tradition before we can criticize it. (122)

The aim is not to dispense with traditions, because some are invaluable for the survival of civilisation and we need to practice conservation of our spiritual and cultural environment in the way that we are now focussed on conserving our natural environment. The objective is not to dispense with traditions but to free ourselves from the taboos of traditions.

> We free ourselves from the taboo if we think about it, and if we ask ourselves whether we should accept it or reject it. In order to do that we have first to have the tradition clearly before us, and we have to understand in a general way what may be the function and significance of a tradition. (122)

To explain the agreement between Popper and Oakeshott it is essential to realise that the "critical rationalism" that Popper defended is not the kind of rationalism that he attacked under the label "comprehensive rationalism" or "uncritical rationalism" in Chapter 24 of *The Open Society and Its Enemies*. From the "other" side, Oakeshott's target was not critical rationalism but the very different, radical anti-traditional position, which Popper also criticized and for which Hayek coined the label "constructivist rationalism". This way of thinking drove the French and Russian revolutionaries to sweep out the old and bring in a new regime of terror.

A residual difference between Popper and Oakeshott was the desirability of active social and political reform. Here Popper was more inclined to activism.

> I am against a challenge to tradition because it is tradition, and in favour of any status quo except where there are good reasons for interference. But I am against the spirit of non-interference and

wait-and-see, and perhaps even complacency, to use a strong and perhaps not quite just term. (Popper to Oakeshott http://www.michael-oakeshott-association.com/pdfs/mo_letters_popper.pdf)

Popper was prepared to advocate active reform, including government action, if it was required to correct a situation that was not likely to "work itself out" in the course of time, like the problems of debt and unemployment in Australia and other places at present. Hayek, the opponent of "constructivist rationalism" and central planning, was prepared to advocate the sweeping away of barriers and he wrote "It would seem to the liberal, indeed, that what is most urgently needed in most parts of the world is a thorough sweeping-away of the obstacles to free growth" (Hayek 1976, Appendix. Why I am not a conservative).

The problem of tradition

Popper encountered the problem of tradition in several ways while he was in New Zealand. One was the absence of a research tradition in Canterbury College and another was the quality of a set of records of Mozart's *Requiem* made in the US by musicians apparently untouched by the European musical tradition. It is likely that some of his ideas about the closed or tribal society were inspired by the Maori tribes, the original inhabitants of New Zealand. He noted some defective parts of the rationalist tradition, such as the metaphysical idea of determinism and also what he called "observationalism", the idea that our knowledge is based on the observations that we make.

A theory of tradition

Now I come to a brief outline of the task of a theory of tradition. It must be a sociological theory, because tradition is obviously a social phenomenon. I mention this because I wish briefly to discuss with you the task of the theoretical social sciences. (123)

As an example of a defective theory he criticised the conspiracy theory of society, that is, the idea that all the undesirable things that happen are deliberately organized by groups of powerful conspirators. Of course conspiracies happen but Popper's point was that they rarely succeed in their plans and intentions although of course the often cause catastrophic damage by their efforts. The outcome of the criticism is his view that the main problems of the social sciences arise from our attempts to understand (and anticipate) "the unintended consequences, and more especially the unwanted consequences which may arise if we do certain things".

Institutions and collectives

Another task of the social sciences is to analyse the formation and function of institutions (police forces, insurance companies, schools) and social collectives (social groups, classes and nation states). This can be seen as an example of the "social" or "rules of the game" theme in action.

The function of institutions and collectives can be analysed in terms of the traditions and the written or unwritten rules that they follow, bearing in mind that the control exerted by rules is plastic (a kind of non-deterministic control that Popper introduced in his lecture "Of Clouds and Clocks", in *Objective Knowledge* (Popper, 1972).

Popper noted that institutions have a very interesting (and dangerous) characteristic which he called the "ambivalence of social institutions". That is the difference between the prima facie purpose of the institution and its actual function (the American sociologist Robert Merton referred to the "manifest" and "latent" function of institutions). Obvious examples are schools that teach unscientific prejudices, police who engage in crime and protect criminals, and politicians who use their position to exploit the public purse and undermine good government to serve factions and special interests.

To illustrate the function of traditions in social life Popper chose the rational or scientific tradition as an example and he described the birth of the tradition among the early Greeks when the members of the school of Thales began to criticize and radically revise the doctrines of the school.

> My thesis is that what we call 'science' is differentiated from the older myths not by being something distinct from a myth, but by being accompanied by a second-order tradition - that of critically discussing the myth. (127)

Critical discussion will raise questions about the problems that the ruling theory addresses, the problems that it does not solve and it will provoke thought about the kind of evidence or observations that will make a difference. This led to what Popper called *the searchlight theory of science*, meaning that our theories act as searchlights, shining into the infinite darkness to pick out or illuminate items of interest in the light of the theory. This stands in contrast to the bucket theory of science (and the human mind) whereby our knowledge is the accumulated mass of material that has been deposited in the bucket.

Chapter 5: Back to the Presocratics

This was the Presidential Address delivered to the Aristotelian Society in October 1958. Bryan Magee described this lecture in *Confessions of a Philosopher*. It was the first time he saw Popper and he was captivated by Popper's account of the pioneering role of the pre-Socratic philosophers in developing the speculative and critical approach to cosmology. Popper described the orthodox school where doctrines are transmitted from generation to generation with the minimum of criticism. An early example was the religious order founded by Pythagoras. There is a story that someone who found a problem in the system, and threatened to tell people about it, was drowned to cover up the scandal. But something very different happened in the school started by Thales, where students challenged their teachers and set forth radical new doctrines without being expelled (or drowned).

Popper claimed that this critical tradition was rediscovered and consciously revived in the Renaissance, especially by Galileo. That led to Popper's most significant thesis, that *the critical method is the true method of science (and learning generally), in contrast to the empiricist and inductivist view that knowledge begins with observation*, and ends up being verified or warranted by reference to sense impressions.

Magee was exhilarated by this head-on challenge to British empiricism and to longstanding ideas about science and the function of observations in the growth of scientific knowledge. He could see that a tradition of several hundred years standing, the empirical tradition, that knowledge starts with experience, was at stake. Popper's method of conjecture and refutation was epic and revolutionary in its implications

> I was intellectually thrilled by the argument... and agog to see it pounced on by this particular audience which contained some of the most distinguished philosophers in Britain most of whom were identified, and identified themselves, with empiricism...I simply could not believe it when, in the question and answer period, not a single person raised this issue or referred to it. The entire discussion, which became impassioned, turned on whether or not this or that particular pre-Socratic philosopher had been correctly represented by Popper, which in turn meant arguing about whether an important fragment might be better understood in a different way. (Magee, 1997, 230)

He went home, nursing his wrath, and wrote to Popper to say that the intellectual frivolity of the gathering was unforgivable but he, Popper, had been partly to blame for presenting his revolutionary epistemology under the guise of a historical study. Popper did something similar in *The Open Society and Its Enemies* so that this magisterial statement of the principles of equalitarian democracy was being widely described as a clever, maybe even brilliant, critique of long-dead scholars, but not a book of contemporary relevance. "He really must stop doing this, I said. His ideas were immensely important, but he was presenting them in a way that almost ensured that they would be misunderstood." (Magee, 1997, 231). A long-running and stormy but rewarding friendship ensued.

Chapter 6: A Note on Berkeley as a Precursor of Mach and Einstein

This short paper lists some of Berkeley's ideas which have a strikingly new look. They were rediscovered and reintroduced into the discussion of modern physics by Ernst Mach and Heinrich Hertz, and by a number of philosophers and physicists, such as Bertrand Russell, Philip Frank, Richard von Mises, Moritz Schlick and Werner Heisenberg.

Popper spelled out the relevant ideas in 21 points, starting with Berkeley's statement "To utter a word and mean nothing by it is unworthy of a philosopher". The second point was "The meaning of a word is the sense-quality with which it is associated (as its name). Apparently that anticipated the verification criterion of meaning of the Logical Positivists. Popper's list indicates how Berkeley supported other "modern" developments in the philosophy of science such as instrumentalism against the idea that there can be deep theoretical explanations of events.

Popper noted that Berkeley and Mach had major disagreements on metaphysics despite the common ground that they shared on instrumentalism. Mach opposed all kinds of metaphysics, especially theology. In contrast, Berkeley was a Christian theologian and apologist. He believed that physics could describe regularities in the world but it cannot find true causes because these are spiritual, beyond the reach of physics, and the "ultimate explanation" is God.

Chapter 7: Kant's Critique and Cosmology

This was a radio broadcast in honour of the 150th anniversary of Kant's death, first published in the *BBC Listener* in 1954. Kant was popular among the general population because he taught the rights of man, equality before the law and perhaps most important, the idea of emancipation through learning, which was a signature idea of the Enlightenment.

> Kant helped to create on the Continent the idea of emancipation through self-education, [which was] hardly known in England where the "self-made man" was the uncultured upstart. The significance of this idea is connected with the fact that on the Continent the educated had been for a long time the middle classes, while in England they were the upper classes. (175 note 4)

Kant and the Enlightenment

It seems that Kant's name and his popular ideas reached the Continent from England in a book by Voltaire which praised English representative government, tolerance and empirical science in contrast with the tyranny and bigotry that prevailed in the rest of Europe.

> Voltaire's book was burnt, but its publication marks the beginning of a philosophical movement -- a movement whose peculiar mood of intellectual aggressiveness was little understood in England, where there was no occasion for it. (176)

Kant was one of Popper's favourite philosophers and he associated him with all the positive ideas of the Enlightenment, and especially with the struggle for intellectual and spiritual freedom. He quoted Kant: "Enlightenment is the emancipation of man from a state of self-imposed tutelage...Dare to use your intelligence! This is the battle-cry of the Enlightenment." (177).

Chapter 8: On the Status of Science and Metaphysics

This chapter contains the text of two radio talks for the Free Radio-University in Berlin, delivered in the late 1950s. These were prepared while Popper was working on *The Postscript to The Logic of Scientific Discovery* and during this time he refined his view of the role of metaphysics in science. This refined view was a radical departure from the dogmatic anti-metaphysical positivism of the Vienna Circle and it led to Popper's theory of metaphysical research programs.

Kant and the logic of experience

This section contains a passage which Bryan Magee identified as the key to locating Popper in relation to the western tradition. In *Confessions of a Philosopher* Magee described him as a reconstructed Kantian and this passage brings that out as Popper agreed although he noted that it was not his intention at the time to make that larger connection with the western tradition (Magee, 1997, 236).

> As Kant puts it: 'Our intellect does not draw its laws from nature... but imposes them upon nature.' While I regard this formulation of

Kant's as essentially correct, I feel that it is a little too radical, and I should therefore like to put it in the following modified form: 'Our intellect does not draw its laws from nature, but tries -- with varying degrees of success -- to impose upon nature laws which it freely invents.' ...We invent our myths and our theories and we try them out: we try to see how far they take us. And we improve our theories if we can. The better theory is the one that has the greater explanatory power; that explains more; that explains with greater precision; and that allows us to make better predictions. ...In this way the freedom and boldness of our theoretical creations can be controlled and tempered by self-criticism, and by the severest tests we can design. It is here, through our critical methods of testing, that scientific rigor and logic enter into empirical science. (*ibid.*, 237)

The irrefutability of philosophical theories

Early in Popper's career he considered that the domain of rational discussion was limited to "scientific" matters but it appears that he changed his position by the time he wrote *Logik der Forschung*. In this section of the paper he demonstrated how philosophical doctrines can be subjected to criticism even though they cannot be refuted by facts. He nominated a number of philosophical theories, all of which he considers to be false:

1. Determinism: the future is contained in the past.

2. Idealism: the world is my dream.

3. Irrationalism: we can sometimes have supra-rational experiences and experience ourselves as things-in-themselves.

4. Voluntarism: In our own volition we know ourselves as will.

5. Nihilism: in our boredom we know ourselves as nothings.

After some discussion of the logic of testing and refutation, he approached his problem: If all philosophical theories are irrefutable, how can we distinguish between true and false philosophical theories?

He then specified three types of theory. (1) Logical and mathematical theories (2) Empirical (scientific) theories and (3) Philosophical or metaphysical theories.

Logical theories are tested by looking for internal contradictions. Decisions in these cases are usually final.

Type 2, scientific theories are similarly tested by the process of criticism and in this case observations can be a part of the critical discussion.

For type 3 problems, he proposed a solution that is based on a "situational analysis" to assess the adequacy of the theory as a solution to a problem. He did not use the term situational analysis in this paper but that is the approach that he advocated in *The Poverty of Historicism* for the social or human sciences. It can be generalized for use whenever we examine alternative solutions to a problem, or the reasons for human actions or the rationality/adequacy of human decisions, such as a Constitutional reform, the elaboration of a metaphysical research program or the location of a shelf in the kitchen.

> My solution is this: if a philosophical theory were no more than an isolated assertion about the world, flung at us with an implied 'take it or leave it' and without a hint of any connection with anything else, then indeed it would be beyond discussion. But the same might be said of an empirical theory...A theory is comprehensible and reasonable only in its relation to a given problem-situation, and it can be rationally discussed only by discussing this relation. (198)

That provides an early indication of the theory of metaphysical research programs which Popper developed during the 1950s.

Chapter 9: Why Are the Calculi of Logic and Arithmetic Applicable to Reality?

This is a technical paper delivered at a symposium organized by the Mind Association and the Aristotelian Society in 1946. At the time Popper was working on a series of papers on "logic without assumptions". He eventually decided that this program was not working although the quality of the work was highly regarded by specialists in the field.

Unlike most of the papers in the collection, this one is likely to have limited appeal for the non-professional reader. Gilbert Ryle's contribution to the symposium was circulated in advance and much of Popper's paper was a response to technical points in Ryle's paper.

Chapter 10: Truth, Rationality and the Growth of Scientific Knowledge

The chapter treats (1) the growth of knowledge: theories and problems, (2) the theory of objective truth and correspondence to the facts, (3) truth and content: verisimilitude versus probability, (4) background knowledge and scientific growth, (5) three requirements for the growth of knowledge.

The growth of knowledge: theories and problems

Popper's aim was to explain the importance of one particular aspect of science, namely, its need to grow, or progress.

> I assert that continued growth is essential to the rational and empirical character of scientific knowledge; that if science ceases to grow it must lose that character. It is the way of its growth which makes science rational and empirical. (215)

He raised the question, whether there is any possibility of science completing its task, achieving the great theory of everything or for some reason ceasing to progress.

> I hardly think so, thanks to the infinity of our ignorance. Among the real dangers to the progress of science is not the likelihood of its being completed, but such things as lack of imagination, (sometimes a consequence of lack of real interest); or a misplaced faith in formalization and precision; or authoritarianism in one or another of its many forms. (216)

He might have added the rise of "normal science", "Big Science" and work in the universities driven by the imperative to "publish or perish", three developments that became serious issues with the mushrooming growth of universities and research facilities after WW2.

His first thesis was that we can specify in advance what would count as a better theory, even before it is invented or proposed. This can be seen as an answer to the Socratic problem of inquiry, often called "Meno's Paradox". Meno argued that we cannot search for what we know (because there is no need to search for it) nor for what we do not know (because we don't know what to look for).

The answer is that we may not be able to specify the details of something that we want for a particular purpose but we can specify the criteria that it needs to meet, including the tests it would need to pass. For example we don't need to specify the design details of a better car engine, but we can specify what would count as improvements like lower fuel consumption, higher power to weight ratio, enhanced durability and ease of maintenance etc.

Popper listed some criteria for the better theory (a list of six criteria can be found in section 3 of this chapter). In a nutshell, the better theory has more content, is logically stronger and it has greater explanatory and predictive power. Hence it can be more severely tested by comparing predictions with observations. "In short, we prefer an interesting, daring, and highly informative theory to a trivial one." (217).

Content and probability

One of the results that emerged is that content is inversely related to probability in the sense of the probability calculus. Of course this is not an attractive idea to those who seek highly probable theories (high p values) but they have yet to produce a helpful and convincing method of calculating the p values of explanatory theories.

Popper noted that his views can be contrasted with the ideal of science as an axiomatized deductive system, a view which he traced from Euclid's Platonized cosmology to Newton, Einstein, Bohr, Schrodinger and Dirac.

> As opposed to this, I now believe that the most admirable deductive systems should be regarded as stepping stones rather than ends: as important stages on our way to richer, and better testable, scientific knowledge. (221)

They are indispensable because we have to test theories by their deductive consequences, which can be quite remote from the core of the theory. To use a concrete analogy, the deductions from the theory can be explained as mooring lines from the "hot air balloon" of science, in contrast to the architectural image of knowledge which has to be built on a solid empirical base like the foundations of a house. For the conjectural or hot air balloon theory of science the empirical tests are not foundations that support the theory but mooring lines that keep in "grounded" with the empirical base.

Objective truth: correspondence to the facts

In this section Popper discussed one of his favourite topics: the way Tarski's approach to truth using the modern theory of levels of language (languages and meta-languages that refer to other levels of language). The correspondence theory of truth can be described as a regulative theory rather than a "terminus theory" of truth. Much talk of truth has the implicit assumption that the truth is a target or destination that we can locate, and approach ever nearer.

Justificationism versus non-justificationism

Popper sketched the difference between the verificationists or justificationists in the theory of knowledge compared with the non-justificationists, fallibilists or critical rationalists and a third group of irrationalists or sceptics (who tend to be disappointed justificationists).

The verificationists demand positive justification of knowledge (usually in the form of subjective beliefs) and they can be called the positivists, in contrast with the critical rationalists who could be called "negativists" because they see logical strength in refutation but not in "confirmation".

The critical rationalists are often criticised as irrationalists and sceptics, with paradoxical views on epistemology (and probability theory) and no serious interest in the truth. Popper attributed that view to the adoption of a justificationist program and the subjective approach to knowledge, two approaches which he rejected.

What makes one theory better than another?

Six indicators that a theory may be preferable to a rival.

1.   It makes more precise predictions and these stand up to more precise tests.

2.   It explains more facts .

3.   It describes or explains the facts in more detail.

4.   It has passed tests which the rival failed.

5.   It has suggested new experimental tests and passed.

6.   It has unified or connected various hitherto unrelated problems.

This paper was written at the high tide of Popper's attempt to provide a formal definition of verisimilitude, that is, a measure to compare the ranking of rival theories in terms of their approximation to the truth. Taking up some of Tarski's ideas he proposed a definition in terms of truth and content. It seems that this topic did not attract much attention until Miller and Tichy pointed out a fundamental flaw in the formula, at which point it the view spread around the philosophical community that Popper's whole program had fallen over.

Background knowledge

Parties to a discussion usually share a great deal of common background knowledge, although any and every assumption can be up for review if it is challenge. For critical rationalists this does not mean that the background knowledge is established, merely that it is impossible to review all the assumptions at the same time.

Requirements for the growth of knowledge

In the last section of this paper Popper proposed three criteria for a new theory to be accepted as an advance in the field.

1.   The new theory should proceed from some simple, new, and powerful, unifying idea about some connection or relation.

2.   Secondly, it must have new and testable consequences; it must lead to the prediction of phenomena which have not so far been observed.

3.   Third, we require that the theory should pass some new, and severe, tests.

Lakatos picked up the need for new consequences of a theory, and the quest for "novel facts" became a major concern in the philosophy and methodology of economics for a decade or two.

Chapter 11. The Demarcation between Science and Metaphysics

This paper stands as a legacy of a debate that engaged the positivists and to a lesser extent Popper over several decades. It was written for *The Philosophy of Rudolph Carnap* in the Library of Living Philosophers series, published in 1964.

Popper's view of the problem

> The repeated attempts made by Rudolf Carnap to show that the demarcation between science and metaphysics coincides with that between sense and nonsense have failed... In all its variants demarcation by meaninglessness has tended to be at the same time too narrow and too wide: as against all intentions and all claims, it has tended to exclude scientific theories as meaningless, while failing to exclude even that part of metaphysics which is known as "rational theology". (253)

Carnap

The *Oxford Companion to Philosophy* states for Carnap that "Technical rigor was the hallmark of his important contributions to formal semantics, the philosophy of science and the foundations of inductive probability". However technical rigor did not suffice to bring Carnap's program to life, as Popper argued in relation to Carnap's demarcation criterion. Popper explained how Carnap's program evolved from (a) his early view on meaning which was heavily influenced by Wittgenstein, through (b) the universal language of science stage to (c) "Testability and Meaning", a 1936 article where Carnap made some Popperian changes to his system but balked at the next decisive steps away from "justificationism" to a full-blooded fallibilism. That was probably as close as they ever came because after Carnap moved on to the foundations of inductive logic there was little common ground.

Probability and induction

In this section Popper described how the full consequences of treating confirmation as if it was just a weaker form of verification became apparent in Carnap's two books on probability. These were more of the same, the appearance of rigor, new terms, tortured arguments, to what effect? Have scientists made any use of Carnap's logic of induction?

It seems that some of the consequences of Carnap's wild goose chase are virtually paradigms of absurdity, presumably due to the mode of thinking that generated the paradox of the ravens discovered later by Carnap's younger colleague, Hempel. For example:

> He [Carnap] proposes that we accept (as probable) a principle to the effect that the evidence 'Sandy is clever' increases the probability of 'A is clever' for any individual A - whether A is the name of a cat, a dog, an apple, a tennis ball or a cathedral. This is a consequence of the definition of 'degree of confirmation' which he proposes. According to this definition, any two sentences with the same predicate ('clever' or 'sick') and different subjects are inter-dependent or positively correlated, whatever the subject may be...I am far from certain whether he has realised these consequences of

his theory, for he nowhere mentions them explicitly. (290)

Chapter 12: Language and the Mind-Body Problem: A Restatement of Interactionism

Chapter 13: A Note on the Body-Mind Problem

These are interesting papers in several ways. Popper adopted the unfashionable position of mind/body dualism and he gave a hint of the important influence of Karl Buhler, his teacher and one of his two doctoral thesis supervisors (the other was Moritz Schlick).

He sketched Buhler's doctrine of the three functions of language: (1) the expressive or symptomatic function; (2) the stimulative or signal function; (3) the descriptive function.

> To these I have added (4) the argumentative function, which can be distinguished from function (3). It is not asserted that there are no other functions (such as prescriptive, advisory, etc.) but it is asserted that these four functions mentioned constitute a hierarchy, in the sense that each of the higher ones cannot be present without all those which are lower, while the lower ones may be present without the higher ones. (295)

A central point of Popper's argument is that the "higher" descriptive and argumentative functions of language involve intentions (for example in naming things) and the intentional or purposive function of language cannot be described as a causal relationship in physical terms.

In view of the obsession with language among philosophers in the 20th century it is surprising that Buhler's theory and Popper's elaboration of it have made practically no impression among philosophers.

Chapter 14: Self-Reference and Meaning in Ordinary Language

A playful piece written in the form of a dialogue between Socrates and Theaetetus. This suggests that Popper could have been very successful as a linguistic analysis if he had dedicated himself to the practice.

Chapter 15: What is Dialectic?

This is one of the first papers that Popper published in English. He read it to a seminar at the Canterbury University College in Christchurch in 1937 and it was published in *Mind* in 1940. He described how the advance of knowledge can be conceived as a trial and error process like the evolution of plants and animals. In a very loose way that resembles Hegel's "dialectic triad" (thesis , antithesis and synthesis). However, contra Hegel and his followers, it is not the contradiction between the thesis and the antithesis that drives the process, it is our efforts to eliminate contradictions.

A minor feature of the paper, in the first footnote, is a comment that defuses one of the common criticisms of Popper's ideas. That is the claim that Popper's falsificationism would bring scientific research to a halt because scientists would be obliged to immediately discard any theory that was apparently refuted, with no excuses, even if there is no better alternative theory at hand. Against that view, Popper wrote:

> The dogmatic attitude of sticking to a theory as long as possible is of considerable significance. Without it we could never find out what is in a theory - we should give the theory up before we had a real opportunity of finding out its strength; and in consequence no theory would ever be able to play its role in bringing order into the world, of preparing us for future events, of drawing our attention to events we should otherwise never observe. (312 note 1)

Chapter 16: Prediction and Prophecy in the Social Sciences

Popper delivered this address at the 10th International Congress of Philosophy in Amsterdam in 1948. With *The Poverty of Historicism* only available in the form of articles in an academic journal he first summarized his critique of "historicism" - the idea that historical studies can deliver prophecies about the future course of history.
He then criticised two other common errors in the social sciences. One is the collectivist or holistic view that the social sciences should focus on "social wholes" or collectives, such as groups, classes, nations, societies and civilizations. Popper defended a form of methodological individualism which does not deny the existence of groups and

collectives but advocates "situational analysis" to take account of the perceptions, plans and decisions of individuals as the explanatory "bottom line" in the explanation of social movements and historical events. Agassi provided a refined account of this position in his paper "Methodological Individualism and Institutional Individualism" (Agassi, 1987).

The second target was the conspiracy theory of social problems which claims that every bad thing that happens is organized by some group of conspirators. He did not deny that conspiracies happen, but they rarely achieve their objectives. As the poet Robert Burns wrote circa 1780 "The best-laid schemes o' mice an 'men. Gang aft agley". Consequently one of the most important tasks of the social sciences is to explore the unintended (and often unwanted) effects of human actions. Popper advocated the approach of the Scottish scholars and Carl Menger who pioneered the study of the evolution of human institutions from that perspective.

He finished the paper with a survey of some modern trends in philosophical thinking, along the lines that the more things change, the more they stay the same. "The historicist revolution, like most intellectual revolutions, seems to have had little effect on the basically theistic and authoritarian structure of European thought." (346).

He suggested that the earlier naturalistic revolution against God only replaced the name God with the name Nature, theological determinism was replaced by scientific determinism and the omniscience of Science. Hegel and Marx put the goddess of History in place of Nature with historical determinism with the sinners against God replaced by criminals who vainly resist the march of History.

But the sequence God - Nature - History did not end there but went on to the deification of facts, the verified facts of logical positivism and then the facts of language and "common use".

Since human behaviour includes verbal behaviour, we are led still

172

further to the deification of the Facts of Language. Appeal to the logical and moral authority of these Facts (or alleged Facts) is, it would seem, the ultimate wisdom of philosophy in our time. (346)

Chapter 17: Public Opinion and Liberal Principles

The paper was delivered at the sixth meeting of the Mont Pelerin Society, held in Venice in 1954. It was published in Italian in 1955 and in German in 1956. It first appeared in English in this collection of papers. As usual when Popper addressed a meeting he wanted to challenge and provoke thought, rather than simply endorsing the assumptions that he shared with his audience. The paper has seven sections: the myth of public opinion, the dangers of public opinion, liberal principles (a group of theses), the liberal principle of free discussion, the forms of public opinion, some practical problems and a short list of political illustrations.

Some basic principles of classical liberalism

1.   The state is a necessary evil and its powers should be kept to the minimum that is necessary.

2.   A democracy is a state where the government can be changed without bloodshed.

3.   Democracy cannot confer benefits on people. Democracy provides a framework where the people have the opportunity to organize themselves.

4.   Democracy does not mean that the majority is right.

5.   Institutions need to be tempered and supported by traditions.

6.   There is no Liberal Utopia. There are always problems, conflicts of interests, choices to be made between the lesser of evils.

7.   Liberalism is evolutionary rather than revolutionary. It is about modifying or changing institutions and traditions rather than wholesale replacement of the existing order. The exception to this is when a

tyranny is in place, that is, a government that can only be changed by violence and bloodshed.

8.   The importance of the moral framework.

> Among the traditions that we must count as the most important is what we may call the 'moral framework' (corresponding to the institutional 'legal framework') of a society. This incorporates the society's traditional sense of justice or fairness, or the degree of moral sensitivity that it has reached... Nothing is more dangerous than the destruction of this traditional framework. (Its destruction was consciously aimed at by Nazism). (351)

On the myth of public opinion, Popper noted that we need to be wary of a number of ideas about public opinion which many people accept without thinking critically about them. He noted the following:

1.   The idea that the voice of the people is a kind of authority, based on the essential wisdom and "rightness" of the mythical "man in the street".

2.   The "manifest truth" theory, which makes people impatient of differences of opinion.

3.   A dangerously irrational and romantic form of the "voice of the people" myth - that the popular will can represent the genius and Spirit of the People.

Moving on to the dangers of public opinion, he noted that it can be very powerful and liberals (wary of concentrations of power and their danger) should treat it with a degree of suspicion: "Owing to its anonymity, public opinion is an irresponsible form of power, and therefore particularly dangerous from the liberal point of view."

> It may sometimes assume the role of an enlightened arbiter of justice. Unfortunately it can be managed. These dangers can be counteracted only by strengthening the liberal tradition. Public opinion should be distinguished from the publicity of free and critical discussion which is (or should be) the rule in science, and

which includes the discussion of moral and other issues. Public opinion is influenced by, but is not the result of, nor under the control of, discussions of this kind. Their beneficial influence will be the greater the more honestly, simply, and clearly, these discussions are conducted. (354)

Chapter 18: Utopia and Violence

This was delivered to the Institute des Artes in Brussels in 1947. Popper noted that the situation in the world at the time was a great challenge to people who hated violence. Despite the defeat of Nazism, Hitler achieved something like a victory in defeat by degrading the moral standards of all the participants in WW2. In addition, the nuclear weapons used to defeat our enemies could end in the destruction of our civilization. But still he saw the attitude of reasonableness as the only alternative to violence in resolving disagreements.

> A rationalist, as I use the term, is a man who attempts to reach decisions by argument and perhaps, in certain cases, by compromise, rather than by violence. He is a man who would rather be unsuccessful in convincing another man by argument than successful in crushing him by force, by intimidation and threats, or even by persuasive propaganda. (356)

In an apparent paradox he suggested that "even a one-sided attempt to deal with others by gentle persuasion" can produce violence if the opponent is a psychopath who interprets willingness to compromise as a sign of weakness. He made the point that two parties are required to make a discussion reasonable. When we are dealing with those who would rather shoot than argue there are limits to reason and to tolerance as well. In *The Open Society and Its Enemies* he wrote that unlimited tolerance must lead to the end of tolerance and we must be prepared to control and limit the intolerant. If we do not then the tolerant may be destroyed, and tolerance with them. (Popper, 1966, note 4 to chapter 7).

> An important consequence of all this is that we must not allow the distinction between attack and defence to become blurred. We

must insist upon this distinction, and support and develop social institutions, national as well as international, whose function is to discriminate between aggression and resistance to aggression. (357)

Chapter 19: The History of our Time, an Optimists View

This was the Sixth Eleanor Rathbone Memorial Lecture, delivered at the University of Bristol in 1956. Eleanor Rathbone was a British MP and a stalwart campaigner on issues including female circumcision in Africa, child marriage in India and forced marriage in Palestine.

At the time of the lecture Popper considered that the optimist's view had considerable rarity value because "the wailings of the pessimists have become somewhat monotonous". This was the height of the Cold War and many people considered that it was only a matter of time before one side or the other precipitated a nuclear war.

As he usually did in his lectures, Popper laid down a challenge to received opinion. In this case he nominated the view that was a cliche of the times, expressed by Bertrand Russell among many others, that our intellectual development has outrun our moral development. "We are very clever but we are also wicked". Against Russell, Popper argued that, far from being wicked, most people are good, "perhaps a little too good, but we are also a little stupid; and it is this mixture of goodness and stupidity which lies at the root of our troubles". (365).

He identified misguided moral enthusiasms as a matter of concern. We are in too much haste to improve the world and there are virtually religious wars between competing theories of how to establish a better world.

> And our moral enthusiasm is often misguided, because we fail to realise that our moral principles, which are sure to be over-simple, are often difficult to apply to the complex human and political situations to which we feel bound to apply them. (366)

Popper considered that (in 1956) there was no need for further criticism of the communist system and he proceeded to criticise the nationalist faith which he regarded as equally dangerous when expressed as the doctrine of national self-determination. This is the idea that the borders of national states should coincide with the locations of particular ethnic groups. There have never (or hardly ever) been nation states of that kind and attempts to shift either borders or people (ethnic cleansing) has caused endless conflict and strife when ethnic minorities demanded that they be allowed to break away or join an adjacent state where they would be the majority. For example Czechoslovakia was formed under the principle of national self-determination but as soon as it was formed the Slovaks demanded to be free (in the name of the same principle), and finally it was destroyed by the German minority, in the name of the same principle. The latest example of this principle in action is the demand for a Palestinian nation state which is used as a rationale for waging war on Israel.

> There are ethnic minorities everywhere. The proper aim cannot be to "liberate" all of them, rather it must be to protect all of them. The oppression of national groups is a great evil; but national self-determination is not a feasible remedy...Few creeds have created more hatred, cruelty, and senseless suffering than the belief in the righteousness of the nationality principle; and yet it is still widely believed that this principle will help to alleviate the misery of national oppression. (368-9)

Chapter 20: Humanism and Reason

This is a critical review to identify the strengths and weaknesses of a book by two scholars, published in 1950 to assert the value of humanism and the humanities against the encroachments of the scientific attitude.

Popper's major criticism was that the authors did not understand the nature and methods of science (at its best) and lapsed into an unhelpful anti-scientific stance as a result.

CHAPTER SEVEN

OBJECTIVE KNOWLEDGE

INTRODUCTION

OBJECTIVE KNOWLEDGE AND EVOLUTION

1. Evolution and the Tree of Knowledge

2. Of Clouds and Clocks

3. A Realist View of Logic, Physics and History

4. Epistemology Without a Knowing Subject

5. On the Theory of the Objective Mind

OTHER PAPERS

6. The Bucket and the Searchlight: Two Theories of Knowledge

7. The Aim of Science

8. Philosophical Comments on Tarski's Theory of Truth

9. Two Faces of Commonsense

10. Conjectural Knowledge: My Solution of the Problem of Induction

Why *Objective Knowledge* matters

It is very necessary these days to apologize for being concerned with philosophy...My excuse is this. We all have our philosophies, whether or not we are aware of this fact [and] the impact of our philosophies upon our actions and our lives is often devastating. This makes it necessary to try to improve our philosophies by criticism. This is the only apology for the continuing existence of philosophy which I am able to offer. (32)

This book revealed significant developments in some of Popper's ideas.

- The twin themes of evolution and objective knowledge.

- The four-stage-problem solving schema which helps to illustrate the synergy of imagination and reason required in the different phases of problem-solving activity.

- A more detailed account of the levels of language which he picked up from Karl Buhler. Popper's account of the role of the descriptive and argumentative functions of language has been surprisingly overlooked by most of the philosophers who took "the linguistic turn" in modern times.

- Some additional aspects of the approach that he called "situational analysis" to explain human action and events. This has two striking features: It helps to heal the artificial rift between science and the humanities that became a fashionable concern in the "two cultures" debate of the 1960s. And it points the way towards a general theory of human action which avoids the reduction of human behaviour on the one hand to purely psychological or biological drives and on the other hand to purely environmental or social factors. - -

The biological approach and objective knowledge

The most interesting feature of the book is the emergence of evolution and "objective knowledge" in five chapters based on papers delivered on various occasions during the 1960s. Bill Bartley described how Popper sprang these ideas on his seminar participants, almost out of the blue, on Tuesday November 15, 1960.

> On that day the members of Popper's seminar had assembled as usual around the long table in the old seminar room on the fourth floor of the old building of the London School of Economics.

When Popper appeared he announced that he would abandon the usual format and would read a new paper of his own. That new paper, which spoke of 'three worlds', of biology, and gave qualified support to Hegel's theory of objective mind, took the members of the seminar off guard. (Bartley, 1976)

The other chapters revisit more familiar themes; conjectural knowledge as a solution to the problem of induction, commonsense realism against the commonsense (subjective) theory of knowledge, the aim of science and Tarski's Theory of Truth. There is an appendix dating from 1948 on "The Bucket and the Searchlight: Two Theories of Knowledge".

From demarcation and induction to objective knowledge

This guide does not follow the sequence of the papers in the book. The five papers on objective knowledge and related themes are treated first, to reflect the title of the book and the most novel contents. The other papers follow in chronological order. This aroused some comments along the lines that the first two chapters in the book, and especially the chapter on Popper's solution to the problem of induction, are fundamentally important and should be treated first.

Re-reading the two papers with fresh eyes, it is clear that those two papers support the theme of objective knowledge by explaining some connections between the problem of induction and the traditional (subjective) theory of knowledge, especially in Hume's influential treatment of the issues. The order of the chapters has not been changed in response to those comments but it may be helpful to indicate how some of the key themes of Popper's work are linked in the paper on induction.

Section 13 in the paper on conjectural knowledge is especially helpful. Beyond the Problems of Induction and Demarcation explains how the solution to the problem of induction came to Popper many years after he produced a solution to the problem of demarcation, possibly as early as 1919. He realized that the idea of falsifiability would make a helpful distinction between Einstein's theory and some parts of Marx, Freud and Adler which were accepted and propagated uncritically by "true believers". At the time he thought it was probably only a matter of definition, and not fundamentally important although he found it helpful to get clear about the best way to use evidence.

Later, when he was seriously engaged with the problem of induction, like the positivists around him, the matter of falsifiability assumed new significance, possibly because the positivists were so dedicated to verification, which he realised would never work, which meant that the quest for justification by way of verification was unsustainable. "I saw that what had to be given up is the *quest for justification*, in the sense of the justification of the claim that a theory is true. *All theories are hypotheses*; all *may* be overthrown." (29).

When Popper considered that he had solved the problem of induction and grasped the close connection with the problem of demarcation, he achieved a "problem shift" to a new range of problems and issues. He became alert to the way that theories can be "immunized" against criticism (with thanks to Hans Albert for the term), and this raised the issue of the social nature of science and the norms, traditions and conventions of the scientific community, which he touched without elaboration in chapter 23 of *The Open Society and Its Enemies* and the final sections of *The Poverty of Historicism*. "Thus I was led to the idea of methodological rules and...of an approach which avoided the policy of immunizing our theories against refutation."

The next step in the evolution of his ideas, as he applied the critical approach to the test statements of the empirical base, was to recognise the conjectural and theoretical nature of observation statements. That in turn led to the recognition that all languages are theory-impregnated which calls for a "paradigm shift" in our perception of the nature of empiricism.

> It also made me look upon the critical attitude as characteristic of the rational attitude; and it led me to see the significance of the argumentative (or critical) function of language; to the idea of deductive logic as the organon of criticism...And it further led me

181

to realize that only a formulated theory (rather than a believed theory) can be objective, and to the idea that it is this formulation or objectivity that makes criticism possible; and so to my theory of a 'third world'. (31)

In the final section of the final paper (in this guide) we can see how Popper's thinking progressed from demarcation and induction to the rules of the game, to theories of language and the ideas of objective knowledge and the evolutionary link between language and critical. As Jarvie demonstrated in *The Republic of Science*, all those themes were present in Popper's first published work and it took a lifetime to draw out some of their implications.

OBJECTIVE KNOWLEDGE AND EVOLUTION

Evolution and the Tree of Knowledge

This was Popper's Herbert Spencer Lecture, delivered at Oxford in October 1961. The paper began with some remarks on "problems and the growth of knowledge" and moved on to methods in biology and especially the theory of evolution.

Problems and the growth of knowledge

Popper noted that he disagreed with almost everybody except Charles Darwin and Albert Einstein. He did not accept the conventional view that we start with observations and build theories on that basis. Instead he insisted that we start with problems that arise when our expectations run into difficulties. At the individual level the expectations are based on our innate propensity to look for regularities. At the level of science and technology our expectations are based on the scientific theories of the time. Our knowledge grows as we work on problems by trial and error in a manner that parallels the Darwinian process of natural selection.

Methods in biology and evolution

Some general theses:

First, there is no royal road to success in science and it is quite mistaken to think that there is a "scientific method" that leads to success.

Second, there is no way to justify scientific results.

> A scientific result can only be criticized, and tested [and all] that can be said in its favour is that it seems to be "better, more interesting, more powerful, more promising, and a better approximation to truth, than its competitors." (265)

Finally, it is essential to criticize a theory in its strongest form rather than setting up a "straw dummy" version of the theory.

A conjecture: "genetic dualism"

The problem is to explain the evolution of very complex structures from random mutations. Popper proposed that this conjecture might strengthen the theory of natural selection, using a generalized historical hypothesis based on the construction of a typical situation (situational analysis). Popper proposed to make a distinction between a behaviour-controlling part of the animal (such as the central nervous system) and an executive part such as the sense organs and the limbs. This is a complex theory and various commentators including Bartley (1976) have pointed out that it is not as original as Popper thought at the time.

Of Clouds & Clocks: An Approach to the Problem of Rationality and the Freedom of Man

The next paper in the series was the Arthur Holly Compton Memorial lecture delivered at Washington University in 1965. Here Popper applied his new evolutionary approach to the old issue of rationality and freedom. He wanted to illuminate the role of plans and intentions in human action, especially the "plastic" nature of that control due to our capacity modify or cancel plans and intentions.

Popper set out to produce an alternative to two opposing theories of human freedom. The first is the determinist nightmare according to which the whole world, including ourselves, is a machine which runs as if by clockwork. In the words of the German poet Novalis this view converts '...the infinite creative music of the universe into the dull clappering of a gigantic mill, driven by the steam of chance and floating upon it, a mill, without architect and without miller, grinding itself to pieces'.

That view destroys the idea of human creativity. "It reduces to a complete illusion the idea that in preparing this lecture I have used my brain to create something new". (222).

An alternative derives from Heisenberg's Uncertainty Principle. Some events at the sub-atomic level happen at random, these random events may become amplified to produce unexpected happenings at higher levels, and so we have the chance to do something original.

Popper did not accept either of those alternatives because in his opinion the real problem is to explain how non-physical things such as aims, plans, values, purposes and arguments manage to exert effects in the physical world. He confronted what he called "Compton's Problem" which Compton discovered after he agreed to deliver a lecture at Yale University at 5 p.m. on November 10th. This decision introduced a kind of plastic control into his movements on and around November 10th. It was not a completely rigid control because the lecture might not have started at the right time and it could even have been cancelled. There was an element of freedom in the situation but it did not derive from chance. What was the nature of this plastic control? How is it that speakers usually turn up on the right day, at more or less the correct time? Popper set out to solve this problem of freedom within plastic control by way of a theory of language in the context of a revised theory of evolution.

The revised theory of evolution is summed up in twelve theses. Among them:

> 1. All organisms are constantly, day and night, *engaged in problem solving*.
>
> 2. These problems are problems in an objective sense. They can

be hypothetically reconstructed by hindsight. Objective problems in this sense need not have their conscious counterpart and where they do, the conscious problem need not be the same as the objective problem. A plant seed has to solve many problems to survive but it is not conscious of any of them.

3. Problem solving always proceeds by the method of trial and error.

7. Using 'P' for problem, 'TS' for tentative solution, 'EE' for error elimination, we can describe the fundamental evolutionary sequence as follows:

P(1) ---> TS ---> EE ---> P(2)

Confronted with a problem, the organism offers tentative solutions; these are subjected to a process of error elimination (natural selection, critical discussion etc) and new problems emerge in the process.

9. This schema can be compared with the Neo-Darwinian schema.

10. Not all problems in this system are survival problems although the earliest problems may have been sheer survival problems.

12. This scheme allows for the development of error-eliminating controls (warning organs like the eye; feed-back mechanisms); that is, controls which can eliminate errors without killing the organism; and it makes it possible, ultimately, for our hypotheses to die in our stead. (242-244)

So much for the outline of the revised evolutionary theory. Popper suggested that plastic control over human activities is maintained with the assistance of language which has emerged, as has consciousness, somewhere along the evolutionary pathway.

Popper's theory of language

Popper distinguished four levels of language. Starting from the lowest these are:

I. The symptomatic or expressive function, which can exist without even a second party.

II. The releasing or signalling function, where communication occurs from a sender to a receiver.

III. The descriptive function which involves naming things. This opens up the possibility of story-telling and this in turn raises the issue of truth vs falsehood.

IV. The critical or argumentative function which occurs in a well-disciplined discussion.

The two lower forms occur in animals (and in machines) and they can occur without the higher functions being present. The two higher forms appear to be restricted to humans; but they do not occur in all human use of language (which can be merely symptomatic or signalling), and they cannot occur without the lower functions being present. Thus one may attempt to reduce all use of language to the lower functions because they are always present while the higher functions may be missing.

Popper suggested that human consciousness, the consciousness of self, is a result of language. In addition, the descriptive use of language gives us access to ideas and abstractions which introduce a degree of control into our behaviour beyond that exerted by instincts and reflexes. That control is exercised within the limits imposed by natural laws which prohibit certain kinds of events and Popper argued that some degree of conscious control, decision-making and planning, are possible because the physical universe is not a closed system but is open to change and evolution.

A Realist View of Logic, Physics and History

This chapter was based on the opening address to the First International Colloquium held at the University of Denver in May 1966. Popper enlarged some points made briefly in "Of Clouds and Clocks"; the evolution of plants and animals proceeds for the most part by the modification of organs or behaviour, while in contrast human evolution proceeds mainly by the development of organs outside our bodies. These new external organs may be tools, weapons, machines and last but not least, ideas.

> Man, some modern philosophers tell us, is alienated from his world: he is a stranger and afraid in a world he never made. Maybe he is: yet so are animals and even plants. They too were born, long ago, into a physico-chemical world they never made...Last came man, who for a long time did not change his environment in any remarkable way...Yet we have created a new kind of product or artefact which promises in time to work changes in our corner of the world as great as those worked by our predecessors...These new products, which are decidedly of our own making, are our myths, our ideas, and especially our scientific theories. (285)

Popper described the four-stage problem-solving scheme and then went on to address some aspects of the growth of knowledge under four headings.

Realism and pluralism: reduction vs emergence

On reductionism vs emergence, the question is whether the sciences can be reduced to physics. It seems that a great deal of chemistry has been reduced in that way but biology remains a challenge, and even more so the world of human consciousness. As a rationalist Popper wished and hoped for successful reduction but he also thought that it was most likely that life would remain as an emergent property of physical bodies.

Pluralism and emergence in history

Moving on to pluralism and emergence in history, Popper started with the history of life on earth and then moved on to the story of mankind which he very largely regarded as the history of our knowledge, our ideas and especially our theories about the world.

> The student of the history of ideas will find that ideas have a kind

of life (this is a metaphor of course); that they can be misunderstood, rejected, and forgotten; they can reassert themselves, and come to life again. Without metaphor, however, we can say they are not identical with any one man's thought or belief; that they can exist even if universally misunderstood and rejected. (300)

Realism and subjectivism in physics

On the topic of realism and subjectivism in physics he examined Boltzmann's theory of the subjectivity of the direction of time and Heisenberg's interpretation of indeterminacy and the lower limit to the effect of the observer's interference with the observed object.

He noted that the Heisenberg formula for energy is usually derived in a complicated manner. In contrast Popper argued that the complicated approach is not necessary because it does not have to be derived from the new quantum theory because it can be derived from Planck's old quantum postulate. On that basis the Heisenberg formulae can be interpreted as statistical scatter relations and are in principle testable.

> Heisenberg himself noted that such measurements are possible, but he said that it was "a matter of personal belief" or "personal taste" whether or not we attach meaning to them;...But they are not meaningless, for they have a definite function: they are tests of the very formulae in question; that is, of the indeterminacy formulae qua scatter relations. (303)

Realism in logic

Defending realism in logic, Popper insisted that he did not look on logic as a kind of game. For Popper, logic is essentially a tool of criticism. It is concerned with the derivation or deduction of truth and falsity through chains of argument. In a valid inference truth is transmitted from the premises to the conclusion. This can be used on so-called 'proofs'. But falsity is also retransmitted from the conclusion to (at least) one of the premises, and this is used in disproofs or refutations, and especially in critical discussions.

The disproof of the premises is the familiar logic of Modus Tollens, the logic of falsification.

He then gave some extended criticism of the intuitionist logic of Brouwer, drawing upon some ideas from Tarski.

Epistemology Without a Knowing Subject

Popper delivered "Epistemology Without a Knowing Subject" at the Third International Congress for Logic, Methodology and Philosophy of Science in 1967. He considered the status of ideas and their implications for us. He rehearsed the "three worlds" theory to argue that human language, in so far as it contains information, belongs to a "third world" of objective contents of thought. He suggested that this approach is important for humanists because it bridges the "two culture" divide between science and the humanities and it also suggests a new way of looking at the relations between ourselves and the objects of our endeavours.

He emphasised the "give and take" in evolution and mental growth between our actions and their results to open up possibilities to transform ourselves, to build on our talents, our gifts and our opportunities. He could have mentioned the opportunities provided by gifted and inspiring teachers, or just people who were there at the right time with encouragement and appropriate suggestions for reading. This chapter runs to 46 pages and covers a very large range of issues.

Three theses

The first is a challenge to the mainstream of philosophy.

> Traditional epistemology has studied knowledge or thought in a subjective sense - in the sense of the ordinary usage of the words "I know" or "I am thinking". This has led students of epistemology into irrelevances: while intending to study scientific knowledge, they studied in fact something which is of no relevance to scientific knowledge...Thus my first thesis is that the traditional epistemology, of Locke, Berkeley, Hume, and even of Russell, is

irrelevant, in a pretty strict sense of the term. (108)

The second is that the theory of knowledge should focus on scientific problems and problem situations, and especially on the critical discussion of rival theories. That approach can extend beyond science to examine social or political problems and their possible solutions.

The third thesis is that studies of the third world of ideas can illuminate the second world of subjective consciousness, especially the thought processes of scientists "but *the converse is not true*" (112).

The starting point is the "three worlds" theory, so it is possible to distinguish (1) a world of solid objects (2) a world of mental states and (3) "a world of objective contents of thought, especially of scientific and poetic thoughts and of works of art."

One of the functions of the three world theory is to challenge "belief philosophers" who are concerned with the justification of beliefs to abandon the quest for belief and focus instead on critical preferences between rival theories or policies, stated in intersubjective or public, (objective) forms.

He offered three supporting theses.

The third world is a natural product of the human animal, comparable to a spider's web.

The third world is largely autonomous, even though it is manmade and exerts feedback upon us.

Objective knowledge grows through interaction between ourselves and the third world, with a close analogy to biological growth and the evolution of plants and animals.

A biological approach

In this section of the paper he elaborated on the way human products, especially knowledge, can be approached in the objective manner by analogy with the study of biological products including behaviour.

The objectivity and autonomy of the third world

One of the arguments for the subjective approach to knowledge is the claim that a book is nothing without a reader. One of Popper's counter-examples is the phenomenon of the book that is not read by anyone or has been computer-generated. It still has contents that are available regardless of the use that is made of them.

An exciting aspect of the three world theory is the emphasis on the unintended relationships and consequences that turn up when you start to pursue problems in a serious and persistent manner. This means "unpacking" the consequences and implications of the theories which are the objects of investigation. For applications of the three world theory, see Champion, 2015 Chapter 7. Agassi developed this idea in a paper on the novelty of Popper's philosophy (Agassi, 1968). He suggested that a person might "be original in being systematic", that is, taking an idea or insight to see how far it will go.

A large part of the objective third world of potential theories and arguments comes about as an unintended by-product of discussion and criticism of the actual books and arguments that are in our hands at present. According to Popper, all of the interesting problems in number theory provide examples. The sequence of natural numbers is a human construction but then combinations and possibilities and problems emerge and these become more complex and more unexpected as we explore this "expanding universe" of numbers.

Language and criticism

Popper spelled out Buhler's theory of the three levels of language and the fourth level proposed by Popper himself. The two lower function of language are (1) self-expression and (2) signalling. These are shared by animals and humans (and even machines). Level 3, description, is a function of the human use of language (with the dance of bees as an interesting transition case) and 4 is the argumentative function. With the evolution of the descriptive function, there emerges the regulative idea of truth, that is, a description that fits the facts. And with the emergence of the argumentative function of language, criticism can be used as a major instrument in the growth of knowledge. For more on language and literary criticism see the essay "Unchanged Meanings" in *Reason and Imagination* (Champion, 2015).

Historical remarks

In this section Popper examined the role of "third realms" of various kinds in Plato and Neo-Platonism, Hegel, Bolzano and Frege. On Popper's interpretation Hegel was a kind of Platonist but the ideas were not fixed and eternal as they were for Plato, instead they are for ever changing; also they are not autonomous, they are conscious phenomena and so are more directly comparable to Popper's world 2 of consciousness. For Hegel there was no provision for give and take between the individual creative element and the world of ideas that is so important for Popper. Bolzano and Frege apparently anticipated Popper's objectivism but did not unpack the consequences in a wide range of applications. Surprisingly Meinong is missing in Popper's story, he did as much as any thinker at that time to explore the idea of intellectual objects of thought which transcend the subjective contents of thought, and physical reality as well, objects like the "golden mountain" which "subsist" without physical existence.

Brouwer's epistemology

Popper wrote several pages in tribute to Brouwer who he probably expected to attend the conference (he died shortly before the event). Popper advised people who are not familiar with Brouwer's intuitionist philosophy of mathematics to pass by this section which goes into some depth on Brouwer's epistemology.

Subjectivism in logic, probability and physics

Here Popper touched on his (then) 35-year campaign against the subjective interpretation of the probability calculus, which he regarded as a capital error in quantum physics.

Discovery, humanism and self-transcendence

The last section is particularly interesting. It seems that for a moment Popper's objectivism was put aside and there was a glimpse of the human being, the "existential Popper" who was capable of making a reference to "the reality of human suffering" in the midst of a tract on quantum physics. He spoke, as usual, about learning by imaginative criticism but he went further than usual.

> This is how we transcend our local and temporal environment by trying to think of circumstances beyond our experience...This is how we lift ourselves by our bootstraps out of this morass of our ignorance; how we may throw a rope into the air and then swarm up it - if it gets any purchase, however precarious, on any little twig. What makes our efforts different from those of an animal or of an amoeba is only that our rope may get a hold in a third world of critical discussion: a world of language, of objective knowledge. (148)

He could have gone further to mention values, aims, objectives and life plans. Charlotte Buhler, the wife and colleague of his great teacher Karl Buhler, had a special research interest in the diaries and life plans of school children. She later became a prime mover in the Third Force of Humanistic Psychology in the US. Popper never mentioned her and so it remains a mystery whether he picked up some hint of the power of life planning from her.

On the Theory of the Objective Mind

The final paper in this series was delivered at the fourteenth International Philosophical Congress at Vienna in 1968. Gunter Zehm reported on this congress in *Encounter* (Feb. 1969).

> Sir Karl Popper rode his hobby-horse and described the mode of "understanding" historical processes as the logical analysis of a historical problem: i.e. as a process having nothing to do with the capacity for empathy. He did this in the course of a paper "On the Theory of the Objective Mind" which can be appropriately described as the real (and only) sensation of the congress...In contrast to all the Utopians and Ideologists at the Vienna Congress,

he said nothing for which he could not immediately produce demonstrable proofs. Nevertheless there was more human hope in his paper than in all the sunny propaganda speeches combined.

In this paper he suggested that psychology may have to be revolutionised by looking at the human mind as an organ for interacting with the objects of the third world. It is important to note that this "third world" theory does not have any theistic implications.

A unifying theme

The theory of problem-solving by trial and error provides a unifying theme that runs through the activities of plants, animals, artists and scientists. It also shows the way towards a general theory of human motivation which avoids the reduction of human behaviour on the one hand to purely psychological or biological drives and on the other hand to purely environmental or social factors. What is required instead is a situational analysis which takes into account, first, the objective problem situation, so far as this can be reconstructed; second, the way the situation is perceived by the participants; and third, the choices and decisions that they make. The analysis must include the ideas, aims and purposes of the actors because these determine which features of the situation are seen as posing the most pressing problem. For instance the Good Samaritan and the people who passed by on the other side of the road confronted the same situation but they selected different problems from it. And when we come to consider aims, purposes and traditions we face the problems that Popper set out to solve in the Arthur Holly Compton Memorial Lecture and his subsequent papers.

Pluralism and the three worlds

This section recapitulates the three world theory. Popper suggested that the mind (world 2) permits indirect interaction between the physical world (1) and the world of ideas. The human mind can "see" tables and chairs, and it can also "see" and "grasp" abstract objects and relationships such as numbers and scientific theories.

> I suggest that one day we will have to revolutionize psychology by looking at the human mind as an organ for interacting with the objects of the third world; for understanding them, contributing to them, participating in them; and for bringing them to bear on the first world. (156)

The objectivity of the third world

Popper argued for the objectivity and the autonomy of the third world, referring to the Stoics as the first to make the distinction between the objective logical content of our communications and the objects that we are talking about.

The third world as a man-made product

The special feature of Popper's world 3, unlike the Platonic superhuman and divine realm of forms or ideas, is that it is manmade. The majority of philosophers consider that ideas are manmade but not autonomous; they are not "real" because eternal verities cannot be manmade.

> I suggest that it is possible to accept the reality or the autonomy of the third world, and at the same time to admit that the third world originates as a product of human activity...[it is autonomous, or superhuman because] it transcends its makers. (159)

The arguments in this section set the scene for the next two sections on understanding (hermeneutics) and the mental processing of the objects in the third realm.

Understanding

This section begins with the vogue of anti-psychologism initiated by Husserl's *Logische Untersuchungen* in 1900 which was probably his reaction to Frege's criticism of Husserl's previous study of arithmetic from a psychologistic point of view. However the kind of anti-subjectivism initiated by Husserl did not last and the humanities persisted with various theories of subjective or psychological understanding as a reaction and a gesture of independence against the idea that they should copy the physicists.

Psychological processes of thought and the third world

Here Popper confronted the school of "sympathetic understanding" or verstehen, or the subjective re-enactment of actions described by the English historian/philosopher R. G. Collingwood. It has to be said that Collingwood is an excellent antagonist because his method of "question and answer", starting with a problem that the actor was trying to solve, clearly anticipates some important elements of Popperian situational analysis.

> As against this [subjective re-enactment] view my thesis is this. Exactly as a subjective state of understanding [is] finally reached, so a psychological process which leads up to it must be analysed in terms of the third world objects in which it is anchored. In fact it can be analysed only in those terms. (164)

Popper went on to use the four-stage problem-solving schema to describe the process of situational analysis that is required to take account of the problem situation and the role of third world elements in defining it and moving on to evaluate alternative solutions.

Understanding and problem-solving

This section and the two following expand on the theme of problem solving with the use of world three objects. He used two examples, one which he described as "very trivial" (a mathematical proposition) and the other is Galileo's theory of the tides.

The value of problems

Here Popper responded to the possible objection that moving the focus from understanding a theory to understanding a problem situation is only shifting the problem, not solving it. The answer is that it is a "progressive problem shift" (a handy term which he attributed to Lakatos) because it leads to more difficult and interesting questions. Moreover this is essentially an active trial and error process. So the answer to the metaproblem of learning to understand a scientific problem is by learning to understand some live problem. "And this, I assert, can be done only by trying to solve it, and by failing to solve it." (181).

Understanding, hermenutics in the humanities

In this section and the next "Comparison with Collingwood's Method of Subjective Re-Enactment" Popper embarked on a close comparison of his approach with that of the subjective school, notably Dilthey and Collingwood.

Part of the problem arises from the defective view of natural science. Students of the humanities do not usually appreciate the amount of "hermeneutics" involved in the natural sciences, that is the process of conjectural reconstruction of problem situations and testing the possible solutions. That is a far cry from the textbook account of observation, induction and verification of the results.

> Labouring the difference between science and the humanities has long been a fashion, and has become a bore. The method of problem solving, the method of conjecture and refutation, is practised by both. It is practised in reconstructing a damaged text as well as in constructing a theory of radioactivity. (185)

The Bucket and the Searchlight: Two Theories of Knowledge

This paper was delivered in German at the European Forum of the Austrian College at Alpback, Tyrol in August 1948. It anticipated many ideas that Popper developed more fully in *Conjectures and Refutations* and it is closely related to the contents of the chapter "Two Faces of Common Sense" and the chapter on "The Aim of Science".

The point was to contest the usual assumption that learning and science involve the collection of sense impressions or data so that they accumulate like water filling a bucket. On the contrary, Popper insisted that the mind functions like a searchlight, exploring the world under the guidance of inborn expectations or, in the case of systematic problem-solving, under the guidance of current scientific problems and theories.

The contrast between the bucket and the searchlight is much the same as the ancient contrast between the mind as a mirror or a lamp. The literary scholar M. H. Abrams wrote a major book on literary criticism *The Mirror and the Lamp* to chart a shift in the "research program" of literary criticism around (1800) from mimetic and pragmatic "mirror" theories to very different romantic and expressive "lamp" theories

The Aim of Science

This was first published in *Ratio* in 1957. It is also Chapter 15 in *Realism and the Aim of Science* (1983), the first volume in *The Postscript to The Logic of Scientific Discovery*.

> I suggest that it is the aim of science to find satisfactory explanations of whatever strikes us of being in need of explanation. That means specifying an explicandum (statements describing a state of affairs) and the explicans (a set of statements that provide the explanation). (191)

Popper offered the apparently paradoxical view that this involves the explanation of the known by the unknown because the phenomenon to be explained is "known" in some sense (a falling apple) and the explanation is usually cast in terms of an invisible cause (gravity).

For Popper, the aim of science is to proceed to explanations of higher and higher degrees of universality, using laws with more content and higher degrees of testability. He rejected the idea that this process can lead to ultimate explanations, an error which he called "essentialism" although his position can be described as "modified essentialism" to demarcate it from instrumentalism. (See the criticism of essentialism and instrumentalism in Chapter 3 of *Conjectures and Refutations*).

Universality and depth

The idea of greater universality implies the desirable quality of depth although Popper suggested that the idea of depth defies exhaustive logical analysis. He explored the condition for depth with the example of Newton's unification of Galileo's terrestrial mechanics and Kepler's celestial physics. He pursued this by indicating the contradictions between Newton's theory and those of his predecessors. The point is that Newton's theory contradicts both Galileo's and Kepler's theories, and so it cannot be derived from them by a process of deduction or induction.

> I suggest that whenever in the empirical sciences a new theory of a higher level of universality successfully explains some older theory by correcting it, then this is a sure sign that the new theory has penetrated deeper than the older ones. The demand that a new theory should contain the old one approximately may be called (following Bohr) the "principle of correspondence. (202)

Philosophical Comments on Tarski's Theory of Truth

This was a talk delivered at the University of California in 1971 on the occasion of Tarksi's 70th birthday.

Popper was a huge admirer of Tarski because in Popper's view Tarski retrieved the traditional correspondence theory of truth using the tools of modern logic and metalanguages. When Popper visited England in 1936 the topic that he most wanted to talk about was Tarski's theory of truth, though he also spoke about the poverty of historicism at Hayek's seminar at the London School of Economics.

He first met Tarski in Vienna in 1934 and during 1935 he saw him again (with others including Godel, and Abraham Wald) in the seminar or colloquium of Karl Menger (son of Carl Menger, the founder of Austrian economics). Tarski explained his ideas on truth in a short private "lecture" on a bench in the Volksgarten, one of the parks near the University.

> Although Tarski was only a little older than I, and although we were, in those days, on terms of considerable intimacy, I looked upon him as the one man whom I could truly regard as my teacher in philosophy. I have never learned so much from anyone else. (322)

In this paper he sketched a program to combine Tarski's theory of truth with his Calculus of Systems to obtain a concept of verisimilitude so that we can speak of theories which are better or worse approximations of the truth. This issue is still a loose thread in the fabric of critical rationalism and some people thought that the whole garment might unravel when Miller and Tyche first located the problematic thread.

Two Faces of Common Sense

Objective Knowledge begins with two long and closely argued papers, the first on Popper's response to Hume's problem of induction, the second with a long appendix devoted to Hume's problem of causation and induction. Chapter 2 chronologically preceded Chapter 1 and is treated first here. This is an expanded version of a talk that Popper gave at his seminar in 1970. The point was to unhook realism from its dependence on the defective (subjectivist) commonsense view of knowledge (the bucket theory). It can be described as a "Cooks Tour" of the range of issues which Popper had on his mind at the time, demonstrated by the number of topics in his research program listed on page 147 of this book. The topics are presented under 32 sub-headings. One third of the paper is "An Afterthought on Induction".

An apology for philosophy

See the motto at the start of this guide on page 180.

The insecure starting-point: common sense and criticism

"My first thesis is that our starting-point is common sense, and that our great instrument for progress is criticism". (34)

At the same time, common sense has been unhelpful in the theory of knowledge because it tends to follow the theory that we learn about the world by observation, by opening our eyes and looking at it.

Contrast with other approaches

Popper contrasted his view with classical Rationalism and Empiricism which both begin with supposedly secure starting points to justify knowledge claims. The starting points are different although both are subjective; psychological sensations for Empiricism versus intellectual intuitions for Rationalism. "Security and justification of claims to knowledge are not my problem. Instead, my problem is the growth of knowledge".

Arguments for realism

Realism and anti-realism are philosophical, or more precisely, metaphysical theories and as such cannot be refuted (a point that Popper pursued in Chapter 8 of *Conjectures and Refutations*). This does not mean that they are beyond argument.

> My thesis is that realism is neither demonstrable nor refutable. Realism like anything else outside logic and finite arithmetic is not demonstrable. But it is arguable, and the weight of arguments is overwhelmingly in its favour. (38)

Popper supported the case with arguments from Albert Einstein and Winston Churchill.

Remarks on truth

Popper rehearsed the story of Tarski's achievement in retrieving the correspondence theory of truth using the tools of modern logic and levels of language (language and meta languages).

> If we want to speak about the correspondence of a statement to a fact, we need a metalanguage in which we can state the fact (or the alleged fact) about which the statement in question speaks, and in addition can also speak about the statement in question. (46)

Content, truth content and falsity content

Sections 7 to 11 treat the truth content and the falsity content of theories, various aspects of verisimilitude and the search for truth. He corrected the misunderstanding that his aim was to beat the positivists at their own game of putting a numerical value on the "value" (in some sense) of a theory. The value that the positivists, logical empiricists and inductivists wanted to quantify was the probability of a theory.

According to this misperception, Popper wanted to quantify the verisimilitude of a theory, that is, to provide a measure that would indicate that one theory is closer to the truth than a rival theory.

> In fact nothing can be further removed from my aims. I do not think that degrees of verisimilitude, or a measure of truth content, or falsity content (or, say, degree of corroboration, even of logical probability) can ever be numerically determined, except in certain limiting cases (such as 0 and 1). (59)

So in response to the question about the purpose of his attempt to define verisimilitude in terms of logical probabilities, he replied that he was attempting to emulate Tarski's achievement (in relation to truth) and demonstrate that it is possible to rehabilitate the traditional or commonsense view that some theories are closer to the truth than others (even if they are false).

John Sceski provided a commentary on the difficulties with this part of Popper's work. Like David Miller, he saw a need for more work and he suggested that "Verisimilitude is not a methodological concept although it is an accoutrement to scientific methodology whose clarification is worth pursuing" (Sceski, 2007, 83).

The mistaken commonsense theory of knowledge

Several sections are concerned with the deficiencies of the commonsense and subjectivist theories of knowledge. The commonsense theory is essentially the "bucket theory" whereby knowledge grows as information flows in through the senses and accumulates, like water in a bucket. Popper suggested that the central mistake is the assumption that we are engaged in "the quest for certainty" (a term that he attributed to John Dewey). However that quest is unsustainable in view of the well documented fallibility of our senses and the theory-dependence of our scientific observations.

The pre-Darwinian character of the commonsense theory of knowledge

Sections 15 and 16 introduce the idea of an evolutionary epistemology after pointing out the pre-Darwinian character of the commonsense theory of knowledge. He attributed the term "evolutionary epistemology" to the American psychologist Donald T. Campbell, and he traced the roots of the idea to some post-Darwinian writers at the end of the nineteenth century - J. M. Baldwin, C. Lloyd Morgan and H. S. Jennings. After some comparison and contrast of the methods of selection as applied to theories and species he concluded that the invention of language, especially the functions of description and argument, enabled a major advance to permit ideas to be eliminated rather than their carriers.

A Cooks Tour of familiar themes

The remaining sections range over a number of issues, each treated in a few paragraphs, a kind of Cooks Tour of several of Popper's familiar themes. This reflects the seminar context where the material was originally presented, presumably to provoke discussion on the many and various problems that Popper was working on at the time. These include the role of background knowledge in identifying problems, the theory-impregnated nature of observations, the method of science and the growth of knowledge through criticism and inventiveness.

An afterthought on induction

After the body of the paper is another Cooks Tour through various aspects of the problem of induction, as it arose from the work of David Hume. At the end is a table where Popper summed up his differences with most classical and modern philosophers on nine points. On the first; others may say "The choice of our starting point is decisively important: we must beware not to fall into error from the very start". In contrast Popper asserted "The choice of our starting-point is not decisively important because it can be criticized and corrected like everything else" (104).

Conjectural Knowledge: My Solution to the Problem of Induction

This paper first appeared in 1971 in the French journal *Revue Internationale de Philosophie*. The opening paragraphs irked many philosophers, including some of his followers, with the bold claim that he had solved the problem of induction followed by querulous comments about the lack of recognition.

> I think that I have solved a major philosophical problem: the problem of induction...However, few philosophers would support the thesis that I have solved the problem of induction. Few philosophers have taken the trouble to study - or even to criticize - my views on the problem, or have taken notice of the fact that I have done some work on it. (1)

First Popper stated the commonsense problem of induction which in his view is based on the defective "bucket" theory of the mind. He then proceeded to dissect the confused and contradictory outcome from Hume's analysis of the logical and psychological aspects of learning from experience. Bertrand Russell summed up Hume's analysis in *A History of Western Philosophy* when he explained that we cannot go on holding to rationality along with the generally accepted views on empiricism and scientific procedures.

> It is therefore important to discovery whether there is any answer to Hume within a philosophy that is wholly or mainly empirical. If not, there is no intellectual difference between sanity and insanity. The lunatic who believes that he is a poached egg is to be condemned solely on the ground that he is in a minority because if the principle of induction is rejected every attempt to arrive at general scientific laws from particular observations is fallacious, and Hume's scepticism is inescapable for an empiricist. (Cited in Popper, 1972, 5)

Popper then embarked on a number of arguments to explain how the theory of conjectural knowledge and the practice of deductive hypothesis-testing provide answer to Hume's problems. Popper's account also conforms to the actual procedures of scientists (and problem-solving in general) much better than attempts to emulate the procedures prescribed by empiricists and inductivists. It helps to remember that Popper described himself as a kind of empiricist, given the critical importance of using evidence to test theories and also a kind of rationalist, given the importance of imagination and insight in generating hypotheses and discovering new problems.

Prompted by Popper, Peter Medawar wrote a critical commentary on the way that papers for scientific journals reproduced the "inductive" approach with the emphasis on the new data and very little consideration of the theoretical problem situation and hardly any discussion of alternative theories and the problems raised by the data. He suggested that papers should start with a statement of the rival theories in the field, then explain how the experimental work was designed to test one or other of the rivals, and then, after presentation of the results, explain how these contributed to the debate, whether they settled any differences and whether they raised any new and interesting theoretical or methodological problems (Medawar, 1964**).**

BIBLIOGRAPHY

Agassi, J. 1964. "The Nature of Scientific Problems and Their Roots in Metaphysics", in M. Bunge (ed.), *Criticism and the Growth of Knowledge*, The Free Press of Glencoe.

Agassi, J. 1968. "The Novelty of Popper's Philosophy of Science", *Intnl. Phil. Quarterly*, 8.

Agassi, J. 1987. "Methodological Individualism and Institutional Individualism", in Agassi. J. and Jarvie I. C. (eds., *Rationality: The Critical View*. Martin Nijhoff.

Auden, W. H. 1941. "Criticism in a Mass Society", in *The Intent of the Critic*, (ed.) D. A. Stauffer, Princeton University Press.

Ayer, A. J. 1936. *Language, Truth and Logic*, Victor Gollancz.

Bartley, W. W. 1964. "Rationality Versus the Theory of Rationality", in M. Bunge (ed.), *Criticism and the Growth of Knowledge*, The Free Press of Glencoe.

Bartley, W. W. 1976. "The Philosophy of Karl Popper, Part I: Biology and Evolutionary Epistemology", *Philosophia* Vol. 6 Nos. 3-4, 463-494.

Bartley, W. W. 1978. "The Philosophy of Karl Popper, Part II: Consciousness and Physics". http://www.the-rathouse.com/Bartley_review_Philosophia_II.pdf

Bartley, W. W. 1982. "The Philosophy of Karl Popper, Part III: Rationality, Criticism and Logic", http://www.the-rathouse.com/2008/Bartley-Part3.html

Bartley, W. W. 1984. *The Retreat to Commitment*, Open Court.

Black, J. 1803. *Lectures on the Elements of Chemistry*, Vol. Edinburgh, p. 193.

Champion, R. 2013. *Aspects of the Duhem Problem*, Amazon.

Donnegan, A. 1974. "Popper's Examination of Historicism" in P. A. Schilpp (ed.) *The Philosophy of Karl Popper,* Open Court.

Firestein, S. 2012. *Ignorance: How it Drives Science*, Oxford University Press.

Friedman, M. 1953. "The Methodology of Positive Economics" in *Essays In Positive Economics*, Univ. of Chicago Press.

Gombrich, E. H. 2003. "Personal Recollections of the Publication of *The Open Society*", in *Popper's Open Society After 50 Years: The Continuing Relevance of Karl Popper*, (eds.) Ian Jarvie and Sandra Pralong, Routledge.

Hacohen, M. 2000. *Karl Popper – The Formative Years. 1902 – 1945: Politics and Philosophy in Interwar Vienna*, Cambridge University Press.

Hayek, F. A. (ed.) 1954. *Capitalism and the Historians*, University of Chicago.

Hayek, F. A. 1960. *The Constitution of Liberty*, Routledge.

Hayek, F. A. 1979. *The Counter-Revolution of Science: Studies On the Abuse of Reason*, Liberty Fund.

Hudson, L. 1972. *The Cult of the Fact*, Harper and Row.

Hutt, W. H. 1951. "The Factory System of the Early Nineteenth Century", in F. A.Hayek (ed), *Capitalism and the Historians*. University of Chicago.

Jarvie, I. C. 1972. *Concepts and Society*, Routledge.

Jarvie, I. C. 1982. "Popper on the Difference between the Natural and the Social Sciences" in P. Levinson (ed.) *In Pursuit of Truth*, Humanities Press, 83-108.

Jarvie I. and Pralong, S. (eds). 2003. *Popper's Open Society After 50 Years: The Continuing Relevance of Karl Popper*, Routledge.

Jarvie, I. C. 2000. *The Republic of Science: The Emergence of Popper's Social View of Science 1935-1945*, Ripodi.

Kealey, T. 1994. *The Economic Laws of Scientific Research*, Macmillan.

Kitcher, P. 1993. *The Advancement of Science: Science Without Legend, Objectivity Without Illusions*, Oxford University Press.

Klappholz, K. and Agassi, J. 1959. "Methodological Prescriptions in Economics", *Economica*, 26: 60-74.

Kuhn, T. S. 1962. *The Structure of Scientific Revolutions*, The University of Chicago Press.

Kuhn, T. S. 1970. "Reflections on my Critics", in Lakatos and Musgrave ,(eds), *Criticism and the Growth of Knowledge*, CUP.

Kuhn, T. S. 1974. "Logic of Discovery or Psychology of Research?", in *The Philosophy of Karl Popper* (ed.) P. A. Schillp, Open Court.

Lakatos, I. and Musgrave, A. (eds)1970. *Criticism and the Growth of Knowledge*, CUP.

Mace, C. A. (ed.) 1957. *British Philosophy in the Mid-Century*, Allen and Unwin.

Magee, B. 1978. *Men of Ideas: Some Creators of Contemporary Philosophy*, OUP.

Magee, B.1997. *Confessions of a Philosopher: A Journey Through Western Philosophy*, Phoenix.

Medawar, P. B. 1964. "Is the Scientific Paper Fraudulent?" https://www.unz.org/Pub/SaturdayRev-1964aug01-00042

Mises, L. von., 1963. *Human Action*, Yale University Press.

Miller, D. 1994. *Critical Rationalism: A Restatement & Defence*. Open Court..

Miller, D. 1996. *Out of Error: Further Essays on Critical Rationalism*, Ashgate.

Mulligan, M., Simons, P. and Smith, B. 2006. "What's Wrong with Contemporary Philosophy?" *Topoi*, 25 (1-2), 63-67.

North, D. 1993 "Economic Performance Through Time" http://www.nobelprize.org/nobel_prizes/economic-sciences/laureates/1993/north-lecture.html

Notturno, M. A. 2003. *On Popper*, Wadsworth.

Notturno, M. A. forthcoming. "Karl Popper in Two Nutshells", in *Proceedings of International Symposium on 'Karl Popper and the Problems of Change' "*, Research Institute for Philosophical Foundations of Disciplines, Ankara.

Parsons, T. 1937. *The Structure of Social Action*. The Free Press.

Popper, K. R. 1957. *The Poverty of Historicism*, London, Routledge.

Popper, K. R. 1963. *Conjectures and Refutations: The Growth of Scientific Knowledge*. Routledge & Kegan Paul.

Popper-Oakeshott letters. http://www.michael-oakeshott-association.com/pdfs/mo_letters_popper.pdf.

Popper, K. R. 1970. "Normal Science and its Dangers" in Lakatos, I. and Musgrave, A. (eds), *Criticism and the Growth of Knowledge*, CUP.

Popper, K. R. 1972. *The Logic of Scientific Discovery*, Hutchinson.

Popper, K. R. 1972. *Objective Knowledge: An Evolutionary Approach*, Oxford University Press.

Popper, K. R. 1974a. "Autobiography of Karl Popper", in *The Philosophy of Karl Popper* (ed.) P. A. Schilpp, Open Court.

Popper, K. R. 1974b. "Replies to My Critics", in *The Philosophy of Karl Popper* (ed.) P. A. Schilpp, Open Court.

Popper K. R. 1976. *Unended Quest: An Intellectual Autobiography*, Fontana/Collins.

Popper K. R. and Eccles J. C. 1977. *The Self and Its Brain: An Argument for Interactionism*. Routledge.

Popper, K. R. 1982. *Quantum Theory and the Schism in Physics*, Hutchinson & Co.

Popper, K. R. 1983. *Realism and the Aim of Science*, Hutchinson & Co.

Karl R. Popper 1985. *Popper Selections*, edited by David Miller, Princeton University Press.

Popper. K. R. 1994. "Models, Instruments and Truth: The Status of the Rationality Principle in the Social Sciences", in *The Myth of the Framework: In Defence of Science and Rationality*, (ed.) M. A. Notturno, Routledge.

Popper, K. R. 2008. *The Two Fundamental Problems in the Theory of Knowledge*, (ed.) Troels Eggers Hansen, Routledge.

Popper, K. R. 2008. *After the Open Society*, eds J. Shearmur and P. N. Turner, Routledge

Sceski, John H. 2007. *Popper, Objectivity and the Growth of Knowledge*, Continuum.

Schwarzchild, L. 1986.*The Red Prussian*, Pickwick Books.

Simkin, C. 1993. *Popper's Views on Natural and Social Science*, Brill.

ABOUT THE AUTHOR

The author grew up in Tasmania. He has a Bachelor of Agricultural Science (Honours) degree (Tasmania and Adelaide), a Master of Arts (Sociology) degree (Macquarie), and a Master of Science (History and Philosophy of Science) degree (Sydney). He has worked as a researcher, policy analyst and editor with architects, engineers and health and welfare agencies.

Further Reading

The Karl Popper Web http://www.tkpw.net/
The website of Rafe Champion http://www.the-rathouse.com
Karl R. Popper 1985. *Popper Selections*, edited by David Miller, Princeton University Press.
Notturno, M. A. 2003. *On Popper*, Wadsworth.

Other Published Books

- *Discrimination and Intellectual Handicap* by Lynne Broad and Rafe Champion, a report on the problems experienced by people with intellectual handicaps and their families, with recommendations for reform. NSW Government Printer, 1981.
- *The Australia and New Zealand Home Unit Handbook* by Rafe Champion, a users guide to the regulations, rights and responsibilities of apartment owners and occupants. Horwitz, 1982.
- *Home Before Dark,* by Ruth Park and Rafe Champion, a historical biography of the boxer Les Darcy, an icon of Australian sport. Penguin, 1995.
- Ebooks. http://www.amazon.com/s/ref=nb_sb_noss_1?url=search-alias%3Daps&field-keywords=rafe+champion

42489660R00119

Made in the USA
Middletown, DE
13 April 2017